Path
of
Duty

Frederick Cornelius

Published by David Cornelius
White Poplars
40 Webb Lane
Hayling Island
PO11 9JE

Edited by David Cornelius

ISBN 978-0-09929649-0-0

Illustrated by Neil Dixon

This book is dedicated to the memory of Frederick Cornelius
and all those who served in the Royal Naval Division in World War 1

ACKNOWLEDGEMENTS

I should like to thank all those who have given freely and willingly of their time, knowledge and skills in the preparation for the publication of this book.

Without the encouragement of my wife, Susan, it is doubtful whether even the first steps would have been taken; throughout, her continuing support has helped to sustain the momentum of this project.

The manuscript text was transferred to tapes, which Susan Surridge patiently and accurately transcribed, working in cross references and footnotes. Her commitment to this long and arduous task, and her very real interest in my father's wartime experiences, I valued highly.

My father's service record was provided by Roy Cornwall of the Ministry of Defence, and he supplied additional information on the location of the prison-of-war camp in Mecklenburg, where my father was held.

In researching the location of the barracks in Folkestone, from which my father embarked for France, I was helped greatly by Keith Rosenz of the Folkestone Tourist Information Centre. He provided information about Folkestone in those war years and took photographs of Marine Crescent where my father was billeted, and of the stone altar mentioned in the text. An extract from the inscription thereon was suggested by Jane Parker as a possible title for the book; it has been used because it reflects my father's high sense of loyalty and duty, throughout his life, to those things that had meaning for him.

The initial layout of the text, research and valuable suggestions on presentation and publication were provided by Carole Dixon and developed by Suzanne Pesics in the limited publication (nominally 100 copies) by Southern Living, Portland in 2000. This present edition of Path of Duty is enlarged by two chapters and photographs of Gustrow PoW. Carole's lively interest in this book inspired her husband Neil to become involved. His artistic line drawings, for each chapter head, skilfully capture the atmosphere and spirit of those days and reflect pictorially the chapter themes.

I would like to thank Norbert Haertle for his hospitality and for showing my wife and I the artefacts, documents and photographs in his possession prior to taking us around the site of the prisoner of war camp at Gustrow where memorials and the large cemetery were still in existence. I am especially grateful to him for giving me a copy of his photograph album, when he visited England in 2007, and I have included some photos in this book.

Finally, my grateful thanks to Nick Barker for his creative ideas, computer skills and suggestions. He reformatted this enlarged edition of Path of Duty as a paperback and as an ePublication, and re-designed the cover. His driving energy and commitment to the task enabled this book to be delivered in time to celebrate the passing of 100 years since the outbreak of World War One.

Each of those mentioned brought a particular and special contribution to this book. Had he lived to see it, my father would have been amazed that the things he wrote about so long ago could capture the interest, imagination and involvement of people whom he never knew - one, two and three generations later.

Chapter headings and occasional footnotes have been added to my father's original text to assist the reader.

David Cornelius

CONTENTS

Introduction

It is not known when Frederick Cornelius wrote this account of his experiences in the Royal Naval Division during the Great War; nor is it known whether he intended it to be published. It is, perhaps, surprising that the manuscript survived the changing fortunes of our family over the past 80 or so years. But, by virtue of its age and survival, it has achieved an added gravitas and a natural imperative that it should be more widely available.

One can only surmise that this account of my father's war service provided the necessary therapy to assist his rehabilitation to the civilian life that awaited him after the horrific experience of trench warfare.

Frederick Cornelius went to war as a young volunteer with a Victorian upbringing, where regular church going and the Christian ethic were impressed heavily on him. He became exposed, rapidly, to an unimaginably different world. This book is his testament to the folly and carnage of war and the adaptability and courage of those caught up in it.

His war began when the combination of zeppelin raids on London, the war situation in France and his sense of duty impelled him, in 1915, to volunteer to fight for his country. He enlisted in the Royal Naval Division and served mainly in horse transport, supplying the trenches with food, ammunition and equipment, and later he fought in the trenches. He saw action as a ranker at Beaumont Hamel, Arras, Gavrelle, Passchendaele, Welsh Ridge and elsewhere.

The Royal Naval Division (RND) was formed originally from the Reserves of the Royal Navy who were surplus to requirements on board ships, but were held on land bases for any special purpose for which they might be needed by the Admiralty. At the outbreak of war in 1914, two Naval Brigades, comprising Anson, Benbow, Collingwood, Drake, Hawke, Hood, Howe and Nelson Battalions, and one Brigade of Marines were assembled to constitute the Royal Naval Division. At that time, this represented a significant addition to the six or so Regular Divisions that were to go to France in the early months of the war.

The RND was used in all the major British theatres of war: Antwerp in 1914; Gallipoli in 1915; Ancre Valley in 1916; Gavrelle, Passchendaele and Welsh Ridge in 1917; the stemming of the German Offensive in March 1918 and the advances on the Hindenberg Line, Cambrai, The Canal du Nord, St. Quentin Canal and near Mons up to the last day of the war.

In all these actions the RND achieved great feats of arms in the forefront of battle and maintained its reputation, despite losses that exceeded three or four times its original personnel.

Throughout the war, the RND proudly retained its naval traditions and practices. It flew the White Ensign, used bells to record the passing of time, naval language to describe activities such as "going ashore" and "coming aboard", possessed naval ranks such as Leading Seaman and Petty Officer instead of Lance-Corporal and Sergeant, allowed its officers and men to grow beards and drank the King's health sitting in the "wardroom".

Attempts to get the RND to conform to Army traditions and practices were tried when General Paris, who led the RND, was wounded. However, his army replacement failed, over a six month period in 1916, to eliminate these naval characteristics. In 1917 the ultimate sanction, attempted by GHQ and the War Office, to disband the RND, failed in the face of effective opposition by Sir Edward Carson, the First Lord of the Admiralty, thanks in part to his political influence. Throughout, the RND fought the enemy on land, whilst enjoying its separate naval identity and successfully defended prerogatives.

The RND exists no more, but its actions in World War I are described in detail and set in a broad perspective in "The Royal Naval Division" written by the historian Douglas Jerrold and published by Hutchinson & Co in 1923. In contrast, this book tells what it was like to serve in the front line as an ordinary seaman in the RND; and of the hopes, fears, attitudes, impressions and comradeship of a young man caught up in (at that time) the greatest conflict in the history of the civilised world - no more, no less than that.

DFC – 2000

ROYAL NAVAL DIVISION

HANDYMEN TO FIGHT ON LAND & SEA

1ˢᵀ BRIGADE

BATTALIONS:

"BENBOW"
"COLLINGWOOD"
"HAWKE"
"DRAKE"

RECRUITS WANTED

2ᴺᴰ BRIGADE

BATTALIONS:

"HOWE"
"HOOD"
"ANSON"
"NELSON"

RECRUITS WANTED

VACANCIES FOR RECRUITS BETWEEN THE AGES OF 18 AND 38

CHEST MEASUREMENT, 34 · HEIGHT, 5 FT, 3½ IN.

PAYMENT from 1/3 per day. · FAMILY ALLOWANCES

Besides serving in the above Battalions and for the Transport and Engineer Sections attached.

MEN · WANTED

who are suitable for Training as Wireless Operators, Signalmen and other Service with the Fleet.

Apply to The Recruiting Office, 112 Strand, London, W.C.

J. MILES & C° L°° Printers, 68-70 Wardour Street, London W.

Reproduced with kind permission of the Imperial War Museum, London

Preface

This book is written as a plain tale of adventures and life in the Great War, 1914-1918. It does not seek to magnify either the comic, tragic, heroic or filthy side of war, but to blend the ingredients as naturally as they happened and try to give its readers a balanced record, rather than a very distorted account.

FMNC

CHAPTER. 1

On a glorious July afternoon in the year 1914, I lay on my back on Seaford Head, gazing through half shut eyelids at the white gulls, swooping and wheeling, diving and climbing, like miniature aeroplanes in the blue vault of infinity.

The low hum of insects, in the sultry air, was soothing, and from over the sea came the booming of guns from invisible ships at practice far out in the English Channel.

The dull concussions persisted and I sat upright; the noise seemed to grow more sinister.

Far away hidden in the heat mist arising from a lazy sea, men were engaged in perfecting the art of destruction.

As the afternoon sun began to dip towards the western horizon I arose and wandered towards the coastguards' station in the hollow between the Head and the Seven Sisters cliffs, and upon nearer approach I could distinctly see a number of soldiers moving about the compound.

"Queer" I thought "for soldiers to be in possession of a coastguard station, I suppose it must be a precaution in view of the reports of unrest and the possibilities of war in Europe"

"War! how absurd on this beautiful summer afternoon."

"Europe! what a long way off. No need for worry, the sea lay between us, and although our press had often written of the possibilities of war, nothing ever came to disturb our island peace."

1: Reverie

On a glorious July afternoon in the year 1914, I lay on my back on Seaford Head, gazing through half shut eyelids at the white gulls, swooping and wheeling, diving and climbing, like miniature airplanes in the blue vault of infinity.

The low hum of insects, in the sultry air, was soothing, and from over the sea came the booming of guns from invisible ships at practice far out in the English Channel.

The dull concussions persisted and I sat upright; the noise seemed to grow more sinister.

Far away, hidden in the heat mist arising from a lazy sea, men were engaged in perfecting the art of destruction.

As the afternoon sun began to dip towards the western horizon,

I arose and wandered towards the coastguards' station in the hollow between the Head and the Seven Sisters cliffs, and upon nearer approach, I could distinctly see a number of soldiers moving about the compound.

"Queer" I thought "for soldiers to be in possession of a coastguard station, I suppose it must be a precaution in view of the reports of unrest and the possibilities of war in Europe."

"War! How absurd on this beautiful summer afternoon."

"Europe! What a long way off. No need for worry, the sea lay between us, and although our press had often written of the possibilities of war, nothing ever came to disturb our island peace."

2: Outbreak of war

Eight days later.

Newsboys shouting "War wiv Germ'ny", businessmen looking anxious, soldiers in London thoroughfares in unusually large numbers and many processions of army carts, limbers, guns and lorries bound for unknown destinations. A strange air of expectancy, not without a little fear, invades the public highways and restaurants and penetrates even into the business houses. England at war and her people could not quite believe the fact. "Business as usual" was the slogan, with its origin rooted in either fear or indifference.

Some people seemed indifferent, some fearful, all a little amazed. Its suddenness robbed all of clear thinking. We, who had been born and reared in a sea-girt land, had not experienced invasion, devastation, broken homes, ruined businesses and loved ones missing; so it was not surprising, even with Germany as our enemy, that the great mass of public opinion believed that with our huge navy and a small expeditionary force, we should soon end the coming struggle. Prophets foretold "peace by Christmas", but omitted to say which Christmas!

Thirty days later....

On the 8.35am train to town, the topics of conversation have changed; instead of discussing stocks and shares, the fastest modes of transport, the latest sport or holiday joys just over, one hears much of guns, soldiers, the German hordes, Mons, the wonderful pluck of our small force in France and the reports in the newspapers. People were buying maps and little flags on pins wherewith to follow the enemy advance.

Newspapers were hurled out of Fleet Street and environs at all times of the day, giving some small fresh item of news from the war zone. These scraps of information were eagerly devoured by men and women alike, but usually with some disappointment at the curt "official" news, which gave but a small glimpse of the position "over there". For instance:

"The enemy today occupied the village of..." really meant:

"Some thousands of lives shattered and bodies mutilated in a grim rearguard action of the British and allied forces."

War correspondents wrote long messages to their Editors but, after the censor had finished his work, little remained for print. The war was shrouded in mystery.

Everywhere this air of mystery persisted; strange comings and goings of men who, at one moment, would be at their accustomed work or business and the next moment missing, leaving behind them the news that they had "joined up". It was going to mean a bigger army than just our gallant little force already heavily engaged, and later our armies to France and other theatres of war were reckoned in millions of men. The lion was not only mobilised, but all his cubs, in the form of colonial battalions, rallied to the call.

The little flags pinned on the maps moved steadily towards Paris and, when it was announced in a bulletin that one of the outlying suburbs of that City had been captured, everyone awoke to the fact that things were serious "over there". This war was not going to be a picnic.

Men, who a few weeks earlier talked of our wonderful army, began to doubt whether this army of ours was going to survive the ordeal of stemming the enemy advance. Wonderful our army had been, even to delay the German hosts, but it came as a shock to the average Englishman to learn that, for the present moment, our army and all its gallant and reckless courage could not stem the tide of invasion, in fact was being faced with a desperate situation of avoiding complete annihilation. Some even hinted that France was letting us down, not knowing that French cavalry gallantly protected our left flank at a time when the Germans threatened to roll it up in a great outflanking movement. Blunders by the French command there may have been, but who did not make blunders at some time in this Armageddon?

3: War on the home front

The war held on and the air raiders arrived. The cowardice of men was shown in its worst light by the killing of helpless women, infants and old folk by night. Terror of darkness became a real menace to most of the fair sex, for they knew that darkness brought the terrifying bombs from Zeppelins hidden in the night sky. Our searchlights sometimes picked them up and the guns barked, but only rarely did they stop a raid. I went, after the second raid, to the Strand and enlisted[1] in the Royal Naval Division.

The German chiefs expected to intimidate with their night Zeppelin raids. Instead of this it only encouraged our people, so much so, that recruiting stations all over the country were unable to cope with the rush to the colours. Perhaps country people missed their menfolk most as in many small towns and villages nearly the whole of the young male population would depart quite suddenly, leaving behind them empty chairs and saddened hearts: Their only consolation was the additional work which fell upon them by the absence of the young men.

Thank God for the work which helped to make the severing of all these ties bearable and pass away the empty days. Eventides always brought the renewal of the sadness when one could only feel more keenly the separation from loved ones. Why did not the Government of every combative nation issue medals for bravery to every wife, mother and lover? Theirs was the courage that went unrewarded. They parted with their menfolk, mostly with a smile on their lips and a wound in their hearts which only made itself apparent in the grief on their faces when the

1. 12 November 1915

beloved ones had departed. The agony of mind seen in the eyes of women, leaving the great London termini after parting with their menfolk, was to call forth all the pity in one's own heart.

4: Enlistment and kitting out

I passed into the small recruiting office in the Strand and was abruptly questioned:

"Age, name, next of kin?" snapped out the Sergeant Major. "Address, occupation and religion?" he concluded.

The details were supplied and the look on his face when I said that I was a clerk left no doubts in my mind that the opinion of my interrogator was averse to my occupation; doubtless he felt, in his soldierly heart, that England was doomed to destruction if she had to rely on such poor material.

"Never fired a rifle before now, eh?" he snapped.

"No sir"

"Don't worry sonny" patronizingly "we'll soon lick you into shape".

I joined a party of 10 more men for despatch to the Crystal Palace to be "licked into shape"; a pleasant kind of torture, where Sergeant Majors, Petty Officers and others watched, while men worked until aching limbs would work no longer. On arrival at the Palace (what irony) we were paraded before the quartermaster's store, and our new clothing and uniform (naval rig) was thrown to us. Being far from expert in the matter of catching things, I speedily found myself surrounded with weird articles of clothing.

Having gathered them together, I retired to a quiet corner to disrobe and emerged from the stores replete in my new outfit. Sailor's cap, two sizes too small; jumper, so tight I doubted my ability ever to be in a position to doff it; trousers, so large that I dreaded tripping over the bell bottoms and boots two sizes too large. Added to this my new vest and pants, well covered with rough hairs, were causing much agony of skin; Nelson's kerchief tied all awry and the lanyard in the wrong place. What a sailor!

We all emerged from the stores in a sheepish kind of way, but within five minutes we were all laughing at each other and at our new appearance. A laugh always helps out a difficult situation. We were formed into a party and marched to our quarters in the main building. The peaceful aspect, which we knew of old, had been rudely disturbed to allow for the military and naval necessities. Statues of nude and semi-nude human bodies of ancient Grecian sculpture, and masterpieces by great sculptors of other countries, had been removed from their position of importance to the dim obscurity of odd corners. Ferns were left to die, fountains were silent, goldfish missing, apparently under a patriotic fervour that had caused them to join up, even if eventually tinned for the benefit of His Majesty's forces. The flowerbeds in the Crystal Palace grounds were in a neglected state and the paths had become weed-ridden. In every building, Canada, Australia, New Zealand, and the Palace itself, hammocks abounded and the places echoed to the tramp of men's stout-booted feet.

The first place I occupied was a hammock in the Main Hall near the Concert Room and a splendid view of the Great Clock could be obtained even after "lights out". My initial attempts at getting aboard a hammock were distinctly disconcerting, but in this I was not alone for several of my near bed-mates were new arrivals like myself. We provided some good laughs to the older hands who cheered us on by calling out ribald remarks such as "Mount her, cowboy", "Mind the bucking bronco", and "Rough sea tonight, sailors".

However, we took it all in good spirit and, after several attempts, succeeded in getting within our hammocks, but having a very difficult time in keeping our balance at the same moment as arranging our blankets. One man, nicknamed "Midge" owing to his short stature, actually fell out again, much to his annoyance, which only added to the hilarity of the watchers. In disgust he slept in his blankets on the hard floor until a kindly offer to "plant" him came from a night guard who held the hammock and at the same time gave him a "leg up".

As I lay very still in my hammock, listening to all the strange sounds around, I felt a bit homesick and this was still more pronounced when lights went out and only the steps of the night guard sounded hollowly along the floors of the Palace. Eventually, the warmth of my blankets soothed me to sleep and I did not awake until the morning guard rattled with his stick on the strings of my hammock, shouting to me to "Show a leg" and "Wakey, wakey, lash up and stow".

5: Training at HMS Crystal Palace

Perhaps it would be well to mention at this stage that I had lost my personal identity and become merely a number, which I was not well pleased about in view of its unlucky tail, it being LZ4013. Added to this indignity was the description of my drill as translated by the Petty Officer. Others being similarly described I did not unduly object, but it became an established fact, among the new recruits, that they would rather fight their PO than the Germans. The personal enmity became greater than the national hatred bred by politicians and press.

Soon I became more expert in rifle drill and joined the Signals school, where the mysteries of Morse code and semaphore signalling were studied. The meaning of port and starboard were made clear and physical jerks, parades and route marches round Sydenham and Streatham were indulged in, until we became hard in muscle and sound in wind. Men stuck to the job really well and, although there were complaints, the dominant optimism of healthy minds and bodies overcame all obstacles.

Our food was generally wholesome, if unimaginative. On one occasion though, cook seemed to have no other idea in his head, or else was unable to obtain anything else, but kippers. Tasty as these are, the appetite is dulled when kippers are served for breakfast, lunch and tea. When they were served yet again for breakfast on the following day Bob Martyn, one of the chaps on my table, expressed his disgust by picking up his kipper and hurling it to the far side of the mess. Within seconds everyone entered into the same, gleefully mutinous spirit. In no time at all, and with much shouting, the air became full of flying kippers. The uproar was soon noticed by the PO who was in the galley with cook at the time. He raced out and quickly restored order, but it was a long time before kippers were on the menu again!

On another occasion, when we were on parade, the PO's stentorian voice ordered "The following men step forward: Frederick, Marcus, Nightingale, Cornelius". I did so promptly, and alone. Almost immediately, the whole parade of recruits dissolved into laughter when they realised that these fine-sounding names were all mine! The PO had lifted the spirits of all of them and I felt that, as the butt of his humour, I had helped. It was in such ways that skilled Petty Officers built up our morale.

There was always a bright corner in the Crystal Palace where the YMCA had their depot and billiards, games of all description, books, writing room, meetings, sing songs and canteen; all helped to make life more interesting and provided a needed relaxation after a strenuous day. I pay tribute to the gentleman and his helpers who were responsible for this YMCA depot; they can be assured that many hundreds of men remember to this day the pleasant hours passed at this centre and, with affection, think of its leader who always considered others before himself.

The picture palace was also available in the evening to those not allowed outside the Palace, and organ recitals and concerts were also given at different periods.

One picture has always remained with me and that was the Sunday morning church service with officers and men in full dress, to the number of about 800, occupying the choir seats around the great organ. The magnificent volume of sound of the men's favourite hymns, "Onward Christian Soldiers", "O God, Our Help in Ages Past" and "Eternal Father Strong to Save", rang out across the quiet vastness of the Palace and echoed, again and again, from the vaulted roof, until the whole place seemed full of men's voices and organ notes. Inspiring, effective, and, we trust, acceptable to our Creator.

6: Training at Blandford

Training proceeded vigorously and soon the raw recruits became a fairly well trained body, with tanned faces and hardened muscles. Visitors were allowed to watch special parades on the "quarterdeck" and it must have been an impressive sight from the top of the steps leading to the grounds, to watch some 2,000 men jump to rigid attention on the stentorian word of command, fix bayonets, slope arms, and march in column of route round the parade ground with smart military step, their bayonets flashing in the bright winter sunshine.

Our Commodore, a tall broad-shouldered man in gold and blue uniform, with the bronzed clean cut countenance of a naval Commander, would be present on the centre balcony surrounded by his officers of lesser rank. He was a man whom one instinctively admired and trusted.

There came a day when a draft was chosen for despatch to Blandford, the final training depot for the Royal Naval Division. I was among the number chosen and my two chums, Bob Martyn and Jack Ferris, were, to my delight, to accompany me. So with some joy, yet not a little regret at leaving the Crystal Palace, we packed our kit bags, returned our hammocks to the store and assembled on the parade ground. The strong voice of the officer rang across the ground, "Parade 'shun; number; form fours; left turn; quick march" and in a few minutes we had entered the station to commence our long journey to the Dorset camp.

The train meandered leisurely through the familiar English countryside and eventually arrived at Southampton, where we were side-tracked for the night, and for the first time I had the miserable experience of sleeping in a cramped position in a third class carriage. Like everything mortal, it came to an end, and with hot tea and sandwiches the early dawn took on a rosy hue; our train shortly met its friend the engine and we were drawn through the Hampshire and Dorset country at quite a good speed for a troop train. We eventually halted at a countrified station and found it to be our destination, Blandford. Within a few minutes we had been marshalled in the station yard and, with a crowd of natives to welcome us, we marched off along the country road leading to our camp on the hills just two miles away.

This camp was composed of well-built timber huts, some even boasted a garden, and in the large parade ground, which stood in the middle of the camp, was the flagmast. The officers' huts, orderly room and quartermaster's stores were ranged around two sides of the parade ground. Situated on a hilltop, with all the beauty of the Dorset countryside in view, this camp must have been a very pleasant place in summer time; but, arriving as we did in the middle of winter, it was very bleak. Washing was a chilly performance and shaving with numbed fingers a difficult task.

Our training commenced a day after arrival and long route marches, trench digging in the hard chalk soil; rifle and bomb practices and mimic battles completed our hardening process. Night operations, the pet abomination of all, were indulged and, although they meant a loss of sleep, we had our humorous moments.

On one occasion the Adjutant was captured by a very ardent patrol whilst attending to nature's needs and, despite his protests, he was not released until an Officer arrived to "identify the prisoner". The Adjutant, irate at first, eventually appreciated the stern devotion to duty of this night patrol when they captured his Orderly in similar manner! On that same night we had to capture a small hill, so in extended order we advanced over the rough country towards our objective. No "enemy" challenged our right to advance and the hill was duly captured without opposition, only it was the wrong hill and our enemy lay on another hill awaiting the attack which never materialised. The Colonel's remarks, duly endorsed by the Adjutant, are better imagined than printed!

On another starlit night we forced our "enemy" to vacate a small wooded hillock. Later we assembled on a nearby road and marched back to camp singing merrily at 1am the popular song "John Brown's Body" but with the soldiers' variations.

Our training at Blandford was very thorough and, as winter gave way to spring and spring ripened into summer, we became very bronzed. As most of us stood between 5'10" and 6'2" in height, were very fit, clear of eye and complexion and well hardened in muscles, it would be hard to imagine a better fighting battalion.

24

In the evenings when we were off duty, Bob, Jack and I, the three inseparables, would stroll down the winding country road to Blandford where we knew a welcome awaited us, either at the church hall, which was open every evening as a club where soldiers might indulge in games and refreshments, or at the house of some friends of my father's family by the name of Best. The good man, his wife and family had ever-open doors to us and many happy nights were spent in their company. The only regret was the return to camp soon after 10pm, but we always consoled ourselves with the thought of the next visit to the town.

Occasionally on Saturdays we would secure a late pass and go by train to Bournemouth where happy hours were spent by the seashore, on the pier and in cafes which gave us an excellent tea for a shilling per head. These visits to areas outside our camp supplied us with that extra refinement and pleasure which we had missed on leaving behind us the old civilian life. Needless to record, the last train to camp was always packed to overflowing with men who had been to Bournemouth for relaxation.

7: Embarkation leave

There came the dawn of a glorious June morning, when it is good to arise early while the dew is still on the countryside and the trees are inhabited by birds of many kinds whose sole ambition seems to consist of bursting their throats with song.

The battalion assembled on the parade ground and we were informed that the first draft to France would be chosen by the Adjutant who came along our ranks and picked out the biggest men. Bob Martyn and I were among the number selected, but Jack Ferris had to secure permission to join us as, owing to his smaller stature, he had been overlooked. We three were very keen on going, as we wanted to have some excitement. The fact that eventually we might receive more than desired did not deter us. Our draft was about 400 strong and we were immediately granted seven days leave.

That leave flew on wings and, before I had almost realised I was home, it was time to report to Waterloo Station. My father, always a silent man, was the first to give expression to his feelings in the warm, long handshake as he bid me farewell, and my mother, smiling, yet with moist eyes, kissed me and wished me God speed. For my own feelings, I will not describe how I felt; only those men who have left home and loved ones to "do their bit" know the agony of parting.

Every man in our carriage compartment sat with flint-like features, trying to hide his emotion, whilst friends said "goodbye and good luck", doing their best to keep cheerful. Several people broke down completely and near me was a young wife disconsolately clinging to her soldier husband.

It was a proud, sad moment when the train departed and we leaned out of the windows to wave a farewell until the distance, and a certain mist in our eyes, hid our loved ones from our view. Tragedy, pathos, sublime heroism, were all too frequently the inhabitants of the great railway termini during the war.

8: Transfer to Folkestone

We arrived at Blandford in the early evening and on de-training I met Bob and Jack. Together we wended our way campwards, talking but little of the war into which shortly we were to be plunged.

We surmised that "over there" it must be rather ghastly, but still strife seemed unreal, situated as we were among the quiet Dorset hills where the setting sun threw its golden red light among the trees and over the fields, where the soft evensong of the birds and the whispering breeze spoke only of peace. We three men, walking along the country lane which led to our camp, were destined to encounter many strange adventures. Though totally unlike in thought, religion and social status, we were united in a common bond for a great object, and we found that bond quite good.

Bob Martyn was a Cockney, rough of manner, blunt in speech, rather crude in expression, yet just the pal to have in a "tight corner". In contrast, Jack Ferris was reserved, refined, with good breeding in every action and a high sense of duty and honour; he loathed his job yet did not flinch. To these two men I was, perhaps, a link and, although we never agreed about any particular subject, yet we remained staunch chums. The army was composed of thousands of like friendships.

Two days were spent at Blandford in becoming fully equipped for active service and we then took farewell of our friends, comrades and familiar haunts.

If curiosity breeds enthusiasm, the "powers in command" played the game to perfection, for no-one ever knew where, when or what would happen next. This secrecy of movement was well-preserved and made army life full of surprises, both pleasant and unpleasant.

We entrained at dusk and travelled all night long to our unknown destination which morning light revealed as Folkestone. We alighted in a very cramped condition, but the fresh morning air soon revived us as we made our way to the "camp" which proved to be the Crescent, a bold semi-circle of boarding houses and private houses close to the harbour. These houses had become devoid of all peacetime comforts, only the floral decorations on the wallpaper gave the rooms an air of late respectability. Around the Crescent and along the beach were barbed wire fences and sandbag walls, which would enable our "camp" to speedily become a fortress, should such a need arise.

"Ain't it kind of the bloomin' War Office to shove us in 'ere without beds" observed Bob slinging his equipment on the floor.

"Makes you feel like a hero, eh Bob?" asked Jack.

"Yus" returned Bob "as much a 'ero as a blinkin' flea in an hempty linen basket".

"Cheer up Bob" I said, "You are well and truly wired around".

"Yus matey, like canaries we are, and p'raps the wire on the beach is to stop the likes of us from swimmin' the bloomin' Channel in full kit".

"Gang int town the neet?" broke in a newcomer to our room.

"What 'opes" sighed Bob.

"Well, let's visit the canteen" I suggested.

Bob became really angry at this point and burst forth "Strike me pink, 'ere we are, ruddy 'eros, doing our bit and only allowed in the bloomin' canteen, when there's scores of pubs outside, 'eaps of pretty "birds", pitchers and good grub. They shoves a ruddy barbed wire fence right rahnd us as if we was pigs and carts us orf to fight the darn' Germins tomorrow without a last fling. Damn shame I calls it".

"Well, we volunteered for it," observed Jack philosophically.

This was too much for Bob who became speechless, a rare occurrence.

"Well boys" I said, "it certainly is different from what I expected. Where are the cheering crowds, the pretty maidens, the bands and flags?"

"Hold hard" chipped in Jack "this is war, not a garden party".

We reached the canteen aided by sounds of singing and soon we all joined in the song that soon became an anthem.

"Pack up your troubles in your old kit bag and smile, smile, smile".

After the last notes had died away, we adjourned to the counter to drink each other's health and as Bob suggested, "Here is to them French hussies". The day dragged on, night came and we retired to our blankets, as we had to make an early move the following morning.

9: Embarkation

We were awakened by reveille at 3am on a chilly June morning, with a fresh wind whipping the sea into foam. Washing and the necessities of toilet being accomplished, we breakfasted on hot tea, bacon, bread, butter and marmalade which was quite a feast compared to the breakfasts which followed. Our equipment was all ready for inspection, so we spent a few minutes after breakfast in strolling along that part of the promenade which lay within our compound.

Half an hour later we paraded, were inspected by our officers, and our draft marched away to the harbour quay where our steamer lay moored. Ironically, it was one of the pleasure boats that regularly ply in peaceful times between Folkestone and the continental ports.

Peacetime! What an eternity away, when one went about one's customary duties without thought of war and hardly a thought of Europe. Yet here we were, gathered from all parts of the British Isles, bound for an unknown destination to wage a bitter conflict with the German youths, many of whom had been quite recently working in our barbers' shops, restaurants and elsewhere. Surely something was seriously wrong with a civilisation, which made, overnight, enemies of men who had been working side by side. Amity suddenly made enmity.

How the Carpenter of Nazareth must have grieved when He observed this wonderful image at death grips after 1900 years of Christianity. Men asked, in their anxiety, "Where is God?" Perhaps God asked, "Where is man whom I made in My image?" What a tragedy.

Our boat, with its human khaki-clad freight, steamed out of the harbour and across the choppy sea to an unknown future of hideous horror. With the shores of England receding, I made my way to the stern to watch the land of my birth fade from view and to see its proud white cliffs softly sink into the mist of distance, eventually to disappear into the horizon like a cloud; I had never left its shores during my life until now. With misty eyes I re-joined my solemn friends amidships and for the next half hour we were interested in the French coast nearing rapidly. We three chums remained silent, each having his own thoughts, perhaps wondering as I did, how many of the men on our ship would re-cross these waters. Even Bob, of ready wit, could not find his voice until we drew alongside of the jetty at Boulogne, and then only to ask for a cigarette.

The grey shadows of destroyers, which acted as our escort, were now returning to the open sea to pursue the faithful execution of their duties as guardians for other convoys. These silent protectors had come out of the grey as we left England's shores and now returned there as we steamed slowly into harbour. We felt proud of these comrades who night and day guarded with quiet efficiency the gateways and passages of France and England. Wonderful work performed daily by our silent service who received little praise for this unspectacular, yet vital duty; tedious at times, dangerous at others, and never relaxing for one moment. Did not England owe her life to its efforts? A soldier of England salutes its sailors.

10: Arrival in Boulogne, transfer to Etaples

Boulogne, seen in the early morning, was unimpressive save for its towering cliffs and the hills in the background, but its houses and harbour and adjoining railway station gave one the impression of business-like practicability. Later, I found its town possessed quaint nooks and old fashioned houses with narrow cobbled roads where one could imagine oneself back in the 18th century. The landing was quiet and the few French people in evidence at this early morning hour only evinced a passing interest in us. They had seen many boatloads of stalwart English lads arrive since the time the first English soldier set foot on French soil. They had seen those same lads, or a few of them, return maimed and broken in the terrible carnage "over there". It was not surprising that some of the older folks looked at us with saddened eyes while we exchanged badinage with a few slightly wounded French poilus.

One old French lady with face framed in snow white hair offered us apples and would not take a penny. When we called her "mother" she seemed very happy. Perhaps her own boys would never again call her by that name or its equivalent "Maman".

We were marched up to our camp on the hills overlooking Boulogne and spent two days there. On the second morning we caught a glimpse of England's white cliffs in the distance lit up by a shaft of bright sunlight. The third day we entrained for Etaples where a huge base camp was situated, and here we were housed in tents near a fir wood.

Bob, Jack and I were early astir next morning and found the camp was very large and covered several small hills. Seaward lay the sand dunes and the base hospital. Southwards, in a hollow, nestled the town of

Etaples; from a distance it presented a charming old world appearance and we were pleased to learn from a friendly Australian that it was not out of bounds at the moment.

We returned to our tents and prepared to shave and wash, but it was a slow business, owing to the distance we had to travel to obtain fresh supplies of water. Before "falling in" for breakfast parade we dived into the woods, which were mostly of fir trees. There we listened to the morning reveille of the birds and watched the glimpses of blue sea and yellow sand dunes which we admired at every break in the foliage.

"What a wonderful place for a camp" remarked Jack. I agreed, but Bob, with an ever-alert mind for possible snags, replied, "Don't be too cheerful old son 'til you've 'ad yer breakfast".

For breakfast and all meals we were accommodated in a large wooden hut with a seating capacity for about 200 men and we found the menu fairly good.

After breakfast came kit inspection, rifle cleaning, and button polishing until our arms ached, then a brisk order was conveyed round the tents to fall in on the parade ground. Assembled on the parade ground were 2,000 men of many different units, including Australians.

After preliminaries, we marched off along the road over the hill, past the convalescent home, to some distant sand dunes with a view over the Atlantic Ocean. Under the few pine trees, which stood sentinel over the dunes, we dropped our full equipment and tunics; with shirt sleeves turned up and carrying only rifles and bayonets we were "put through it", charging over the sand hills and then sticking our bayonets into dummy Huns. The Sergeant Major was relentless and under a hot sun we speedily became a mass of perspiring humanity.

A short rest at 11.15am and we were at it again, this time capturing innumerable sand hills by brief rushes in open formation. Then later we indulged in rifle drill and, at 12.30pm, we were ordered to double to our equipment, dress and "fall in" on the road. The remarks of Bob, and in fact most of us, are better imagined than recorded.

Day after day, under the blazing sun, we had similar work and, if we were not tough enough after this treatment, nothing on this earth would have worked the miracle. Our only consolation was the fact that after tea at 4.30pm we were free to go to the camp's cinema or down into Etaples. Once Jack suggested a walk over the dunes to watch the shipping and Bob promptly told him where to go, only it wasn't a pleasant place.

So we spent our evenings in Etaples in the first comfortable estaminet we could find and, seated in easy chairs, would while away the time with cards, drinks and smokes. Jack could always obtain the very best seats as his good knowledge of French made the inhabitants very friendly disposed towards us; and if Bob had not been so tired out at the end of each day, we should have had difficulty in restraining him from going off with "one of them pretty French tarts".

The town of Etaples was a quaint place with its air of antiquity, its cobbled roads and its peaceful byways. Only the advent of the war and the arrival of the British Tommies had lent to it a new life of bustle and prosperity.

There came a day when our draft was paraded with towels to go sea bathing at Paris Plage, a very pretty resort a few kilometres from Etaples. The entrance to the town lay along a broad, tree-lined avenue, past ornate houses painted in various colours, which, showing in glimpses through the green of the trees, made a pretty picture. A tall lighthouse, standing like a sentinel in the midst of the town, would at night broadcast its welcome light over the sea to warn mariners of the treacherous sand dunes abounding along the coast.

We reached the beach, a smooth sandy stretch, very firm and inviting, but instead of being crowded at this time of the year it was deserted but for a few elderly ladies and some very old men. One realised by this view of a French resort that the nation was very busy indeed in its death struggle with the enemy.

On reaching a quiet part of the beach we undressed and, not having any bathing costumes, dashed into the sea in our nudity, like a company of Neptune's returning to our element. After a great deal of fun in the water we came out prepared to re-join our clothes when a number of pretty French maids came tripping along the beach and barred our way. They were offering to sell us chocolates and cigarettes. Although feeling very awkward we managed to make our small towels conceal a fair amount of our bodies and the boldest spirits bartered with them while the rest of us dressed. Even Bob was not a little disconcerted.

The girls were quite unconcerned and, judging by the rapidity with which they sold their merchandise, the move was evidently well thought out and was the means of effecting sales.

"Well, well" ejaculated Jack, while putting on his boots, "these French girls are expert saleswomen, but rather embarrassing".

"Just the thing Bob appreciates" I re-joined.

34

"Not much" said Bob "the other way round for me".

"Hope we come again" exclaimed Jack rising to his feet.

We all laughed at this wish being expressed by such a very sober individual as Jack and for a long time afterwards he was chaffed about it, until he eventually fell in love with an English nurse.

Our men, wherever they went, soon became great friends with the French; only in comparatively few instances was that friendship taken advantage of, so that the love French girls gave too freely to the fresh, young looking Englishmen ended in serious consequences. Too much was made of these exceptions for in wartime, when restraints are removed between men and women, certain it is that some will indulge and, although this is to be regretted, it is a source of satisfaction to know that the great majority of men knew how to behave towards the women of allied nations.

After this outing at Paris Plage we returned to camp in good humour and indulged in open-air boxing matches in the evening. During one match an adversary connected with a hard straight left to his opponent's chin and knocked him out of the ring into an adjoining lavatory which was merely a pit dug into the ground. The laughter, which greeted this misfortune, was hilarious and we all retreated very speedily to make way for the unfortunate combatant to go to the baths. After this event the boxing ring was shifted to another part of the camp, well away from the lavatories.

Bob and I had many bouts with Jack but he, having acquired an expert training at his college in peacetime, would mostly have the better of the argument, despite my extra reach and stature and Bob's superior muscles. Bob and I were very evenly matched, the usual result going to each alternately. The only time Jack Ferris was beaten was by a bull of a fellow who once held some Indian championship. The whole of our draft turned out to see the match and they had plenty of thrills for Jack was game to the end of a ten round contest, although Bob had to spend half-an-hour in "putting his face straight".

On occasions I loved to stroll up to the hillcrest near our camp and view the sea and sand dunes by moonlight and think for a while of home, loved ones and friends, while the light breezes caressed the pines which crowned the hill. Peace was here, though, in the hollow beneath, agony was endured by the patients in the base hospital. Life in the miniature, peace and pain side by side, joy and sorrow interlinked. On the hilltop serenity and grandeur, with a silver path across the ocean where the moon greeted the waves, while a short distance away men were lying in agony in shell craters, gasping their life away in the light of the same moon. Strange, but it was life.

11: Transfer to the fighting zone

It was on a humid July morning in 1916 that we were informed that our draft was under orders for the "front". Mostly the news was accepted with pleasure as so many months had been spent in training that we were all fed up and the move into action would be a diversion. Full kit inspection followed the announcement, deficiencies were made good, ammunition was issued, gas helmets renewed and soon we were in A1 fighting condition. The rest of the day was devoted to cleaning up camp and speculating on our destinations.

Early next morning after breakfast, we paraded, were addressed by the camp Adjutant, and then marched in column of fours to the railway station where we entrained for an unknown destination. Our train consisted of a long boiler type of engine used mostly for fast goods trains, 18 closed cattle wagons and a first class passenger carriage for the officers. On the floor of each wagon was a liberal covering of straw and plastered on the outside were various remarks in chalk, such as "Non-stop Berlin", "Room for 20 pigs", "Allemand Express" and "Blighty Special", which had been scrawled by wags who had previously used this train. "First Class Pullman" also ironically appeared on several wagons and an irate passenger had carved on one door "The Lousy Limited".

The train started at a walking pace and never accelerated throughout the whole journey so we were able to alight at many places en route and pick flowers with which to adorn our trucks or collect wood and make fires for the boiling of water for tea.

The countryside through which we passed bore a striking resemblance to Essex with its peaceful farms, undulating fields, orchards, woods and rivulets. France was not at war in this corner of her territory.

The evening dusk settled at last upon the land, and as the bright reflection of the sun on the clouds died away and the stars appeared, Jack Ferris, standing at the door smoking a cigarette before seeking his billet in the straw, suddenly called me to his side and pointed away to the east.

"There they are Fred".

"There what are?"

"The Bosche".

"You mean those gun flashes?"

"Same thing".

"Well Jack, what of them?"

"Thought you would be interested to know you are getting near the line".

"Yes, I am". A silence.

"Bit uncanny ain't it?" said Bob at our backs, he having awakened from a sleep to find us interested in that flashing in the eastern sky.

"Very uncanny".

"If this train stopped, I bet you'd hear the rumble of the guns".

"Most likely".

A sharp bend in the line somewhat hid our further view and we therefore composed ourselves for a few hours sleep upon the hard floor of our wagon.

The sharp grinding of brakes eventually roused us and we stretched aching limbs before getting up to open the sliding door of our truck. The sight, which greeted our eyes, I shall never forget. The whole of the near horizon was lit up by brilliant flashes throwing into relief the trees, farms and cottages near us; a continuous trembling rumble was heard, distant yet ominous, like the early stages of an earthquake or a coming summer storm. Every few minutes brighter flashes would appear and the rumble would become a distinct boom or crackling sound, evidently some of our heavy guns coming into action.

The whole earth and sky seemed to be pulsating.

It was magnificent, yet numbing, and one or two in our truck looked scared. Perhaps we were all surprised by what we observed, for it was our first view of massed guns in a night tirade. The train jerked itself into action again and Jack, pointing out to the eastern sky, dramatically exclaimed "Well boys, there's the inferno, here comes the fuel".

"You cheerful idiot".

"Stow it".

"Put him to sleep someone".

"Shove a sock in it".

These remarks having silenced him, the occupants of our truck began a heated debate as to the distance between our train and the front trenches. The estimates varied from 10 miles to a mile, but doubtless, if the law of average were applied, it would have been fairly correct to say five to six miles away. Our train had many halts during the next two miles and it gave us the impression that it really did not matter if any soldiers or war stores ever reached the front. This modern war was certainly not a speedy affair at this stage. We were all train weary, dirty and hungry so we looked forward with eagerness to the final stop. It came at last, and a military policeman came along the line to warn us to stand by for dismounting.

We appeared to be very near the battle front at this point for the Verey lights could be clearly seen rising and falling and in their falling showing up the smoke of battle laying like a mantle over the earth. One reflected on the fact that these lights had been rising and falling and the guns pounding away their death knell for close on two years. For two years - two long, agonising years men had stared with blanched faces at those lights, had crouched near the earth when they burst, had waited through each minute of each day for what? A blinding crash and unconsciousness, or relief, which unstrung the nerves too quickly?

Yes, all this had happened, and was still happening, even while we looked at this awe-inspiring pyrotechnic display. Men were still dying. Two years of death. Jack Ferris broke the silence within our truck.

"Funny how the gun flashes and lights seem to describe a semi-circle around the horizon, almost as if the Germans were holding us in huge pincers and only a very small avenue of escape".

"Yus, does look like it from 'ere" answered Bob "but I expect it's only the lights wot gives it that look".

"You're probably right Bob" I chipped in "look at those lights over the farmhouse and those at the end of the platform, much nearer aren't they? So it is possibly only deception caused by the long distance the lights are visible. Anyhow, pincers or no pincers, we're in it for better or for worse".

What a choir the guns made from the sharp bark and rattle of the smaller ones to the diapason of the "heavies", terrible in their roar. In the brief moments of quiet we could hear the rat-a-tat of the machine guns and the crack of rifles. The immediate countryside about us seemed hushed and quiet, as if listening to the chorus.

It was quite a relief to our thoughts to hear a human voice shouting, "Get out and line up on the platform". Our officers quickly formed up the draft and, with the aid of electric torches, led the way from the dark station to the still darker road that led in the direction of the guns.

No street lamps, no lights in house or cottage windows, nothing but black figures moving in a starlit blackness, with only a sharp shaft of light from passing cars lighting us up with ghostly beams. This part of the country seemed to have escaped the ravages of war for the trees and hedges were untouched, and the cottages, farms and houses appeared to be intact. We passed one or two small villages whose inhabitants, if any, were fast asleep, judging by the absence of lights.

The march lasted nearly two hours and our final halt was in a cobbled square of a mining town, apparently used as a base for troops in reserve from the trenches. The large guns were booming just outside the town, presenting to the enemy a chance to strafe both guns and town on the excuse of searching for the batteries.

We were divided into various groups and escorted by the Town Major's assistants to different streets and billeted in houses devoid of furniture, but intact in walls and roof, so that with the aid of blankets and ground sheets we made ourselves fairly comfortable upon the floors. The more energetic of our number lit candles and produced packs of cards which, together with a few bottles of beer, helped to while away a merry hour until our officer, calling upon us, insisted on our going to sleep. One by one the candles were blown out and soon slumber enwrapped us.

Our officers, meanwhile, were having a drink with the Town Major before retiring to their quarters, an old large house facing upon the square. A tribute to our officers was made by a rough mining engineer from the north of England in these words: "They're not bad chaps, always tuck us up before going to bed themselves". It was this fact of our officers personally seeing to the welfare of the men over whom they had command, which strengthened the ties of goodwill and comradeship and made men follow their officers into the most hellish places, regardless of personal danger. The German officers, being more aloof and autocratic, did not kindle in their men any real regard other than that enforced by discipline, whereas our officers, in the main, were considered "good sports" - a tribute to be proud of in wartime.

12: Petit Saens and trench repairs

"Get up yer lazy devils, there's some French 'tart' artside" shouted Bob excitedly next morning, giving Jack and I a kick to arouse us, finally, from the warmth of our blankets.

"French girls" ejaculated several voices at once, and we were soon all crowding at the one dirty window to find without a number of females of all ages engaged in filling buckets, kettles and other receptacles from the water taps which stood on the kerbs at varying distances along the street. Houses had no internal water supply in this town and the street taps supplied all needs and made, at the same time, a meeting place for the feminine population to exchange the latest gossip.

We were surprised to find the town inhabited by so many civilians as, when we arrived at night, most of the houses appeared to be empty. It did not take us long to dress and run outside, there to fraternise with the fair water carriers and to offer our services in the carrying of water. We laughed with them, tried to make them understand our school French, but mostly it was a failure, and we had to resort to signs and the few words common in sound to both French and English. This, however, is apt to cramp one's style.

We ascertained, by using Jack Ferris as interpreter, that the town was named Petit Saens and was used as an advance base for the "line"; also that all its menfolk, except the boys and very aged men, had been called away on active service. Bob wanted to know if this was an invitation to take the place of their own men, but, when Jack obtained the answer from the fair "femmes" it was to invite Bob to "carry their water every morning".

Not what Bob had wanted but, gallant Cockney that he was, he agreed to carry out their suggestion.

After a wash and shave, we three meandered round the town and found the mines had been rather severely damaged by shell fire, but that very few of the houses had been hit, though quite a number bore marks of combat in broken windows and shrapnel-scarred walls. The women-folk and boys mostly worked in catering for the troops billeted in the town or for a meagre existence in the surrounding fields, quite ignoring the ever-present danger of sudden shelling from enemy guns.

The side of the town nearest the line had suffered most of all, but no damage was found on the western outskirts and only the noise of distant strife broke the peacefulness of this country mining town. At 11am we had to parade, but were immediately told to dismiss for the day and commanded to "make and mend", which meant clean up equipment and rifle, darn socks, sew holes in shirts, clean boots or polish buttons. Unofficially, it meant card games, draughts, visits to cafes and estaminets and doing what one fancied within certain limits.

All of our draft were very pleased as, when we came into the town at night, we little expected that daylight would bring us such delights in a town where tempting articles of food could be bought and charming girls kissed. A most important point for the welding of international friendships was the way "Tommy" everywhere made himself friendly with the fair sex; yet only in a comparatively few cases exceeding the bounds of friendship and making girls sorry that they had given their friendship too willingly.

The day passed pleasantly and night brought her rest, and another day its exercises and the next night its first journey up to the line; not as a fighting unit, but armed with spades and shovels as a digging party. Jack Ferris, being on guard, was not one of the party.

The sky was clear and starlight gave us enough illumination to discern our surroundings. The guns were quiet and only an occasional sharp crack from a sniper's rifle gave indication of the position of the two hidden hosts who faced each other in stubborn conflict. The Petty Officer in charge of our party led the way along the main road to Bully Grenay, a small town in which troops were held in immediate reserve. Although within easy reach of enemy guns, which day and night reduced slowly its number of houses, there still remained open a few estaminets run by civilians. These men and women had, however, taken the precaution to dig large shelters or dugouts under their houses so that a certain amount of protection could be obtained when desired.

We marched along the main road and then turned into a communications trench just as a French battery opened up and sent a salvo of shells over the German lines, as a salutation, to bid the enemy "good evening". This rather displeased us for we did not want the artillery indulging in a little private quarrel of their own while we were engaged, in unprotected positions, rebuilding shattered trenches. However, our batteries, getting no reply to their message of hate, relapsed into silence after a few more rounds and the evening sky grew dark in a silence, which could almost be felt - the strange, uncanny silence which only a battlefield can produce.

After interminable windings our party arrived at the support lines and a new experience had begun for most of us. A halt, and whispered consultations, led to our moving about 20 yards further into the front line of trenches and, as we filed past the sentries whose heads were a silhouette against the starry sky, we observed how intense was their watchfulness. Those sentries might have been cut in stone for all the movement they made. They had that intent look, as though they were trying to see right through the blackness of night to the German trenches. It was eerie, the intense quiet; the darkness, except for an occasional Verey light which only increased the strangeness of our surroundings by its ghastly glow leaving an even greater blackness when it expired. The silence was relieved only by the swish of flares, the occasional crack of a German sniper's rifle or the sharp rattle of the Lewis gun. It was a frightening experience, but nevertheless preferable to a strafe, or so thought the working party.

Another halt, another whispered consultation, low mutterings, then a loudly whispered "forward" and we eventually reached our destination - a trench that had been blown in during a bombardment. We began rebuilding this shattered trench that German meinenwerfers (a large shell fired by trench mortars and particularly damaging when the range was accurate) had despoiled of all semblance of its former shape. Bob whispered to me "Don't like the look of this" when he unearthed a box of live Mills bombs. With a cool nerve he picked up the box and took it to the Petty Officer in charge; the wonder was that the contents did not explode after the shaking received as it needed only one pin to work loose to end the career of Bob and perhaps wound a dozen others.

Sandbags were filled with earth and a new trench wall was built; the party was told to "get going". So, with this first brief visit to the trenches, we had started to take a real hand in the war business. When Bob reached his billet he found Jack reading and so broke out with "Call yerself a ruddy soldier, why you ain't been in the trenches yet, and didn't we git it 'ot ternight, I tell yer we had a job to make ourselves 'eard with the noise of them bloomin' shells bursting". Jack, who had noticed how quiet the night was, asked if they had been issued with a ration of nuts, which drew forth from the others a laugh at Bob's expense.

Bob and Jack then went out to find some wood and returned a little later with some fuel with which a fire was lit, dixies put on to boil and soon everyone was having hot coffee and biscuits. Cards were produced and mild gambling was indulged until 2am with a little singing thrown in to keep everybody cheerful. Then someone trod on a candle and smashed it; thus ended "night operations" to the relief of the losers and the chagrin of the winners.

13: Trench warfare

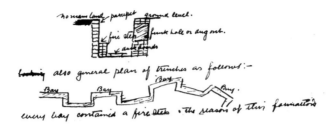

The next day the Royal Naval Division came out of the trenches for a brief rest and then the draft was divided up into the various battalions whose names are household words in English history. Drake, Hawke, Hood, Howe, Nelson, Anson etc. were names of battalions and keen, friendly rivalry existed between them. We three friends were placed together in the Howe battalion, much to our satisfaction. Our company officer, Lieutenant Maynard[1], was a "real gent", according to Bob, and much beloved by the men under his command. We new men mingled freely with the old hands and learnt that the sector we were in at present was "quiet and cushy". Three days rest, which rest always included inspections, re-equipping and working parties, passed quietly.

Once again the Howe battalion marched to the trenches. We passed one battery of French artillery on the way. This battery opened fire and somewhat startled some of us by the sudden sharp reports. We were soon to be quite used to gunfire, and its effects, before many weeks were over. We entered the trenches to the right of Bully Grenay and dusk was creeping on so that by the time we had reached the support line it was practically dark.

Jack, Bob and I were told to get on the fire step and keep a sharp lookout. We were in "fighting order equipment" which consisted of web equipment, water bottle, bayonet, ammunition, rifle, greatcoat, groundsheet and haversack. The full packs had been left in a store in Bully Greenway. We proceeded to "make it 'omely" and Bob fixed up a

1. Douglas Jerrold (see further reading list) records that Lietenant Maynard was killed on 13 October 1916 in the Battle of the Ancre whilst leading his company in the attack on the third German line.

waterproof sheet so as to make a sort of covering for those off duty. There was also a small "funk" hole or dug out at the back of them and every bay contained a fire step. To those readers who did not see the trenches, the sectional diagrams[1] will be of interest. The reason for this formation of trenches was to avoid large loss of life when a shell made a direct hit. Only the men in a particular bay would stand the full shock, the other bays would be sheltered; whereas if one long straight trench were made it would mean that the shell, when bursting, would have a wider destructive area and also would help the enemy in getting the range more effectively.

We three were in the support line and were, therefore, looking out over the front line about 30 yards away. Bully Grenay acted as a reserve line. The only thing to disturb the serenity of the first night was a violent thunderstorm that severely tested Bob's newly erected groundsheet. He was lying underneath it on the fire step, with me alongside, and we kept trying to cheer Jack with enquiries as to his health. He, being sentry, muttered imprecations on our heads and obtained what shelter he could from his steel helmet. The collapse of the groundsheet, with contents of mud and rainwater, on to Bob and me somewhat amused Jack, but we could not see the joke. We had to transfer to the "funk" hole, which was too small to be comfortable, and sleep was snatched in a sitting position with chins nearly touching knees.

The next morning broke in a blaze of sunlight; I breathed deeply of the sharp air and felt it good to be alive. The lark rose on high and I admired the "lucky little blighter" who could bring such sweet song to this land of desolation and yet escape when necessary.

After a frugal breakfast, Jack and I were put to work on a digging party for a sap to the left of our present position. This sap, running from our front line towards the German lines, gave us an excellent opportunity of observing the lie of the land without being observed as some bushes were growing immediately alongside.

To the rear was a now deserted factory building and Jack said he "thought it very sad to think that only two years ago young French girls and fellows must have been going to their daily duty, undisturbed by any fear of the future, and would wander, after work was over, in the pleasant fields which were now seared with trenches and ploughed by shell bursts".

1. At the chapter head

46

Happy girls and fellows, where are you now?

Are you girls working in munitions factories?

Are your lovers lying on some battlefield, looking up with unseeing eyes? "Take cover," shouted the Petty Officer in charge and the next moment a blinding flash and crash nearly caught our working party. Then some of our French mortars got busy and soon the sap was the centre of activity, so much so that a temporary retirement at the double was necessary to avoid loss of life. When the strafe died down, the party resumed labours and Jack and I were able to further observe. In the distance was the mining town of Lens at present occupied by "Jerry"; to the front lay fields and small copses broken by shellfire and trenches. Everywhere in the danger zone trees were bare or nearly so; they seemed stricken as by a storm or blight and made a very dreary landscape. Huge oaks and elms, which, before war came, lifted proud heads to the sky and provided homes for birds, now were lifeless, stark, bare trunks. Otherwise, everywhere seemed peaceful and only occasional gunfire in the distance or the crack of a sniper's rifle told of death. "Yet a thousand men are waiting on watch just opposite us" I observed "and an army buried out of sight only in the next field; seems very uncanny, hardly believable".

"Yes, seems sort of unreal," commented Jack.

Away to the right lay Vimy Ridge hidden in heat haze, almost as if nature had placed her shroud over it to hide the past, present and future from the eyes of all. That ridge, which was so important as a strategic position, had cost already thousands of lives and would cost thousands more. So nature, on this day, hid this deathbed from sight.

The sap had been strengthened and the party left; tonight further digging would be done. That night the enemy bombarded our trenches with whizz-bangs and shrapnel. The whizz-bangs, small shells but very sharp in landing and report, are fearsome things at night when the suddenness of them caused men to flinch and get nervous. The overhead burst of shrapnel usually caused some loss of life and reduced the morale of the men. Some loss of life and wounds were the outcome of this night onslaught and for the first time I saw a dead man on a stretcher, body and head covered with sacking, only feet showing; it turned me sick at heart to think that only five minutes ago this broken body was a living being like myself. Some mother, all unknowingly, had lost a son; some wife a husband; some lover left disconsolate. Such is war! Several wounded passed down the trench, glad they were alive with only a "Blighty" wound. Still a desultory fire went on and our guns opened out in reply.

"Stretcher bearers at the double" rang out a cry in the pitch-blackness, lit only by the bright flashes of guns and the enemy's flare lights. Some men rushed along and soon another "broken reed" was carried away. Eighteen casualties were recorded that night in what was only a minor operation, a mere whim of some artillery officer to see if the enemy was awake.

"Glad we're not out wiring tonight, 'eh Jack?" "Yes Fred".

"Well Jerry's iron rations 'ave come and none for us - 'aint yer disappointed?" asked Bob.

"Can't say I am" from Jack.

"Well you damn well orter be, a Blighty one for me says I, and not too big an 'ole to sew up either" grunted Bob.

"Want jam with it Bob?" I asked.

"No! But I am fed up wiv this war any old 'ow, only 'free days is quite enough, wiv Jerry gettin' more savage every hour" replied Bob.

"Poor old sod" chipped in another fellow and the conversation dropped. Yet Bob Martyn was no coward, only he preferred his old life, as did the huge majority.

A head bobbed in the dug out and a voice shouted "Cornelius, Martyn, Ferris; fall in at the end of this trench for ration party".

"Well I'm blowed if we ain't clicked again," groused Bob. "'Ere all day 'ard at work, includin' being shot at and then got to fetch yer bleedin' grub, nerve eh?".

The journey consisted of wandering round one trench, up another, along another and then on to the ground level where a light, hand-propelled railway truck brought up the food in sandbags from a dump in Bully Grenay. Three journeys were made before the job was finished and by this time it was about 1am; we were dog-tired and simply flung ourselves in to the dugout and fell asleep, unworried by anything except an occasional rat, a big ugly fat one, that would persist in sharing the dugout to the discomfort of the inmates. Rats were numerous and after a time men became hardened to them, but at first it caused annoyance and repulsion. Sometimes the officers would go rat-hunting at night and many rodents were killed during these attacks, the method being to find two holes, plug one with a smoking rag and wait outside the other with trenching tools, sticks etc. to cosh them as they appeared. Some officers even had revolver practice and shot several.

The following day passed without incident and the Howe Battalion was relieved that night and went into reserve at Bully Grenay.

Next day it was good to get a bath, consisting of showers in the back portion of the building, which seemed to have been at one time a Town Hall or municipal office. After the bathing parade, dinner, consisting of heated MacConochie stew, was quite palatable after cold bully beef and fatty soup. Then came the most important parade of any, namely pay parade, and what a joy to receive the 15 francs which were soon expended in canteen, cafe or estaminet.

The next time (if there is a next) a war comes along, the best way to popularise this most dangerous job would be for the Government of the day to pay men according to the nature of the work performed. Thus, instead of munitions workers at home getting fabulous wages while the soldiers had a miserable pittance, the reverse should be the case. It might also prevent trouble if the same conditions prevailed, as for instance:

> desertion - penalty death
> neglect of duty - penalty death
> disobedience of orders - penalty death

Why in the name of Justice should these rules be made for our fighting men while workers at home had to be visited by our leading statesman and implored to produce shells and yet more shells? Our men at the front were being shot at like rabbits for want of adequate artillery protection. Another thing the soldiers wanted to know was why many businessmen and traders at home were allowed to get rich quickly at the expense of their dependants? It would have given our men greater pleasure to show their skill with the rifle against our profiteers than against the Germans. The enemy, in this respect, were far superior to us.

14: Sunday sustenance

"Look out, Jerry above us" shouted Bob and there, sure enough, up in the blue vault of heaven were several enemy bombers being engaged by our anti-aircraft guns. The white balls of smoke appeared to be all round them and among them, but the planes continued on their way, apparently bent on mischief at some large camp or town well behind the line. They had hardly disappeared before a single plane hove in sight, acting as spotter for the German artillery, and soon an exchange of compliments was taking place between the guns on either side.

The next moment, one of our "sausages" - our observation balloons - was brought down in flames by the German plane and the observer descended safely by parachute. That evening two of our planes went over and brought down the enemy balloons. Such is war!

On Sunday came the pleasure of the church service which gave to those attending some little comfort in the midst of war, and turned men's thoughts for the time being to nobler and far more certain things than war. The sing-songs, which took place in Church Army and YMCA depots all over France, were something to remember, and the old hymns seemed to spring to life when sung by men who were daily facing death. To those who went there, and there were hundreds of thousands each Sunday, the time was spent very happily and when minds were stretched to breaking point and hearts were overwhelmed, then these sing-songs, with a short service following, were like oases in a dreary desert. Men seemed to become once more softened and brotherly and, when one realised that the Germans were doing likewise, this war seemed so foolish with all its killings and maimings. The loved ones at home seemed very near at these services. Although only tables and benches, and sometimes a limber as pulpit were used, such services brought keen memories of the Sabbath days before the great madness broke over Europe. The Padre was a Scotsman, beloved of the troops, and much wonderful work he did among the men. Wherever men needed him he was found; often in the front line he went to cheer, comfort and console. His influence was sadly missed when he was at last sent away for a rest and recuperation.

To the people who sneer at and criticise religion, let it be pointed out that but for the example of its preachers and of the remembrance of its Founder, little hope would have been left in men's hearts and still less of love. Even to men of no religious belief, there existed a certain faith in the little pocket Bibles that were issued to them; they were kept in their breast pockets and sometimes read surreptitiously, and when caught in the act they would excuse themselves by saying there was nothing else to read. Yet behind this excuse lay a world of yearning in their hearts and even some of the roughest characters began to take a definite interest in the Hero of all time.

15: Jack is wounded

A glorious summer evening, the sky flecked with fleecy clouds, the sunset growing fainter, the eastern sky rapidly darkening and the stars beginning to appear, almost shyly at first then growing bolder, brighter. As the western sky became duller it found the Howe battalion again preparing to enter the trenches. We did not have any fear as we walked up the long communications trench, for were we not hardened "old sweats" having already experienced our baptism of fire and been in "No man's land" on wiring parties and patrols?

Silence almost uncanny rested on everything, not a gun barked, not a rifle cracked, only the dull booming in the far distance and the sound of men's equipment rattling. Suddenly it was as if all hell were let loose and guns of all calibre, rifles, machine and Lewis guns, kept up a perfect orchestra of hate from both sides.

The earth trembled, men's faces blanched, orders were shouted and the cry for stretcher-bearers was heard. All wild life disappeared, more gaunt tree trunks fell, more gaps appeared in the earth, shrapnel rattled on men's helmets and corrugated dugout tops, and over the earth spread a mantle of smoke lit by flashes of fire - indeed an awe-inspiring scene if one could have looked at it in a detached and danger-free manner. As it appeared to most humans, it was terrifying and frightening. Bob Martyn and I were sheltering in a funk hole in the junction of the support and communication trench awaiting orders when Jack shot in to the accompaniment of a terrific crash of a heavy shell a few yards off.

"Blimey, soon blew you in, too proud to know yer ole pals until Jerry taught yer some manners" growled Bob.

"Shut up Bob, lend a hand, Jack has copped a packet"

"Garn Fred 'e ain't 'urt only winded".

Jack lay gasping and suddenly Bob realised his pal was really hit so we lifted him to a sitting position, found a jagged sleeve and blood streaming from a bad gash in the arm.

"Poor kid" I said. "Does it hurt much?"

"Not much" Jack gasped, "Its numb, lost use of my arm".

I used the first aid packet every soldier carried while Bob gave Jack a sip of "water" from his bottle - only the "water" had something strong in it. "Good 'eh?" asked Bob. Jack nodded thanks, laying back to rest and looking very shaken and white. Bob wriggled out of the hole and once again the familiar "stretcher bearers" was heard, and then after a minute "stretcher bearers, yer lazy, lousy swines, where are yer?" The bombardment was dying down and the stretcher-bearers were fully busy but at last the help arrived and Jack was carried down to the first aid post.

"Poor old sod" sympathetically from Bob "only two of us now Corny boy, 'ave a fag".

"Thanks, I feel pretty fed up losing Jack; somehow I knew we three couldn't last long together in this country but I hope his arm doesn't have to come off. Plucky he was too, not a murmur while I bandaged, only a gasp or two".

"'Ope he loses his arm, it'll keep 'im out of this bleedin 'ole anyway. I'd swop a bloomin' arm to save me body, and I'd give me arm to the rats as a ruddy compensation for not gettin' me 'ole body" commented Bob between whiffs of the comforting cigarette.

"Forward, Howe men" came a voice "and turn down Shaftesbury Avenue" (a trench rejoiced in that name) and we once again got busy.

Later it was learned that four men of the Howe battalion were killed and 22 wounded. "Not a bad cop for Jerry, the bleeder" was Bob's summary "and in a quiet sector too. 'Opes I don't strike a noisy one". After a quiet night the morning revealed a somewhat battered trench as a result of the previous night's "fireworks". Here and there a corpse, or part of it, was showing and caused the living occupants of the trench to shudder in horror, or joke to hide their feelings, or accept as a casual sight. One arm was wearing the French uniform, for our gallant allies had fought many severe battles here; in another place a German head and breast were exposed, and in another a Frenchmen's leg. Can you people who were at home realise these things, because they were part of the life at the front?

Perhaps it was well that these things were hidden from dear ones at home, yet I would like to take by the throat all warmongers in every country and show them these things and make them look, and look, and look until they doubted their sanity, even as we who went sometimes felt ourselves losing our mental balance with the horror, the hopelessness and the grief of it all.

Tell the coming generations about war, real naked war, unvarnished, with the heroes cut out of it and they will see a stinking, horrifying thing, loathsome, unfit for men who think, and they will see to it that the world in their generation does not commit itself to this madness. Young men and women be convinced, war is hell and no rules or regulations can make it good. It is relieved only by the heroism and sacrifice which men and women displayed from being absolutely debasing. Even the horses engaged would stare with fright in their appealing eyes, hot breath in nostrils, sweating, quivering in fear at this atrocity which their "superior" masters were committing. If ever another war must come, in pity's name, leave out all dumb animals, they do not deserve such a fate and should not know and witness men's "civilised" actions.

16: Jack falls in love

Jack Ferris was taken from the dressing station by ambulance to the first field hospital and, after an operation extracting a splinter from his arm, he was taken by train - one of our GER corridor expresses converted into a hospital on wheels - to the Etaples base. There he was placed in a nice clean bed with sheets and blankets, a luxury, which he had not enjoyed for some months, it seemed years. A pretty and charming nurse hovered round him, taking temperature, re-dressing the wound and generally playing the part of ministering angel. "What lucky chaps we are" remarked Jack, sighing with content. "Some are and some are not, you have escaped without losing a limb" replied nurse "but in the next hut we have some poor dears who are in a bad condition".

"Well Sister, there's a lot of talk about equality in this war, but that's impossible as Jerry doesn't deal out his gifts equally. Anyway, I'm jolly glad my arm is saved and that you are going to be near me".

Sister Ruth flushed slightly at his tone and hurried away to another case just arising where a leg had been amputated. Jack began to take an interest in his surroundings to take away thoughts of the pain all down his arm. The next fellow to him appeared to be asleep, the one on the other side was groaning slightly, one lower down was talking rapidly in an Irish brogue to his next bed mate and further along a poor chap was vomiting from the effects of chloroform. Still fresh cases came in and the ward was soon filled.

Another trainload arrived and the weary surgeons had to find fresh strength and nerve for these additional cases. As the Chief Medical Officer remarked to his junior "It's not surgery, it's pure butchery;

hacking away limb after limb, sewing, slicing, cutting, injecting, until the heart sickens of it all". Indeed the life of an MO was every bit as arduous as the trenches and at times they were worn out and sick with the horror and persistency of their work. No blood tingling thrill of battle to make them grit their teeth and go in to win, only this everlasting nightmare of knife work. The nurses too are able to command everybody's esteem and admiration for the stubborn fight with disease and broken bodies. Only the care and grit of this cream of English women pulled many a soldier through.

Sister Ruth Carrington was only a young girl of 21 years when she took up the heavy burden and right well she fulfilled the menial duties which at first befell her, until her chance came to go to France when she was soon second in charge of the ward. Her deft fingers, cheerful disposition and tireless energy endeared her to the men who passed under her care and also earned many a word of appreciation from the doctors. Even the ward Matron, a stern disciplinarian of the peacetime army hospitals, gave her an occasional cheery word of commendation. This Matron, stern and dutiful as she was, had a heart of gold and that gold sometimes showed itself when a particularly exhausted staff needed a relief very badly. Many were the times this stern middle-aged Matron did duty for 20 hours of the day in order to give rest to a sadly overtaxed subordinate.

Ruth Carrington was a beautiful girl, daughter of a Rector, corn coloured hair, blue-grey eyes, an oval face, sweet lips made to smile and a perfect skin. Hands were dainty, figure slight, but supple and she could boast to 5'8" height. It was no little wonder that Jack found himself watching for her appearance and closely following her every movement. He loved her voice, well cultured and low, and was jealous of every word given to the others in the ward.

One morning she came in with the mail and handed him a letter saying "Here you are Jack, a letter from your best girl".

"Oh no!" he protested "not a girl, but my dear old Mater. Do you know Sister Ruth I haven't a girl to write to me; will you?"

"Perhaps" she smiled and was gone.

The next morning Sister Mary brought him a letter that brought the blood to his face and caused his hand to tremble when opening it. It read:

"Dear No7,
Just a little letter to a lonely soldier boy to say someone is thinking of him and longing for his speedy recovery".

Girl-like it proceeded with:

"Will you be pleased when you are able to get to Blighty for leave? I shall miss you very much No7, you have always been so patient and easily pleased, although at times you have addressed me in a way that is not strictly permissible according to hospital regulations.

"How your dear Mater will rejoice when she sees you once again and I expect you will be so happy you will forget your nurse.

"If you are very good, you may take me to Etaples next Saturday as I am off duty at 3pm and it will be goodbye.

"I shall have to wish you very good luck then and I shall dread to think of your return to the Front, though I know you will be always brave wherever you roam. My sincere wishes and God bless you.

Yours very sincerely

Ruth Carrington"

His heart was beating fast with joy at the thought of this girl giving him some of her precious off-duty time and he determined it should not be "goodbye". He did not reply by letter but when next she visited him, whilst he was sitting in an easy chair by the fire, he whispered "Thanks Ruth, I am looking forward to next Saturday more than any other day in my life". Up to the present he had always regarded girls as a rather necessary evil and he was often cynical in his attitude towards them. The sole exception was his mother whom he loved dearly. Now, however, another woman was creeping very surely into his heart and affections. Her nobility, good breeding, loveliness and great patience attracted him and he began to believe in a good God, and a little of his cynical outlook on life was vanishing.

The happy day arrived and with his arm in a sling and his heart beating rapidly he sought out his love, and together they walked to Etaples and wandered amongst its quaint paved roads and alleys and purchased a few articles needed for daily use in addition to some of the fancy things which the French delight in.

"Shall we have some tea Ruth, I'm starving, as well as thirsty?" asked Jack. "Let's" from Ruth with her eyes on a dainty cafe opposite. They established themselves in a bay window with an old window seat, raftered ceiling and late summer roses in an ornate vase on a Louis XIV table. They were served with a liberal tea of scones, cakes, pot of tea, and fruit;

conversation suddenly ceased and both were feeling a little wistful for soon Ruth must return to her duties and Jack to England, later to return to stern duty.

A party of Australians from the camp nearby strolled along singing and making the most of a few hours of freedom. Some English soldiers passed with several French girls arm-in-arm. The westering sun shone through the window making gold patterns on the wall and lighting up the gold in Ruth's hair so that she appeared radiant. Jack spoke in a low whisper "Ruth dear, do you care for me?" She turned her face to him and in her eyes he read her answer. Quite simply she asked "Why Jack?" "Because I love you dear" he answered in a strange husky voice. She smiled and came closer and before he realised it he had his arms about her and was caressing her hair and whispering sweet names, but did not kiss her. He felt quite unworthy in that moment.

"I shall miss you very much Jack dear".

"My love, pray for my safe return to you, I can't pray for myself" he confessed "and I shall want to come back to you, it has made life very precious, your love for me".

She shuddered slightly and promised him that she would always pray and think of him. Perhaps the sights she had seen of men crushed, bleeding, broken, suddenly made her afraid for him for she surrendered her young body to him in an ecstasy of love and yearning and kept kissing him on the cheeks and mouth.

At last she raised misty eyes to him with a request. "Shall we say "au revoir" now, I shall be afraid to trust myself at the station and it will be a better farewell Jack?"

"Yes Ruth dearest, but surely I may see you when you return to hospital - between your spells of duty".

"Why yes, Jack my love, but before my next long spell you will have gone".

He sighed and held her closer until the good French lady proprietor came to clear away, when they departed radiantly happy to purchase a ring as pledge of their love. This Ruth proudly wore, and that night men in her ward marvelled at the sweetness of his nurse and knew not the reason.

17: Resting, re-equipping and return to the trenches

Meanwhile, the Royal Naval Division had withdrawn from the trenches and was resting in quiet country towns and villages well back from the front line, engaged in reorganising, re-equipping and undergoing special war training, testing in gas chambers the new type of helmets which had been issued, doing parade drill, and taking courses in signalling, Lewis guns and many other things so as to be fully prepared for the task ahead.

This task, namely an advance in the River Ancre region, was to test the division to the uttermost, for it was already early autumn and heavy rains would soon render the battlefields well nigh impassable. However, the men, with great traditions to uphold, were quite undaunted and everywhere the spirit of the troops was good and made the responsibility of the officers comparatively light.

Coming out of an estaminet at Hersin, Bob and I sauntered back to the barn that was our temporary home. The night was starlit, but low clouds scudded across the sky and presaged rain.

"Well, ready to move tomorrow Bob?"

"Yus, Corny old chappie, time we did another bit o' scrappin'; gettin' paid for nuffin' lately!"

"What about a hand of cards when we get back?" I asked.

"Righto! I'm game" said Bob "but early to kip tonight, reveille at 5 o'clock tomorrow".

Back at the barn other occupants were already busy playing and we joined in with modest stakes, until the Petty Officer came in to give final instructions for the morning. We drank up the remains of the beer and laid our blankets in the straw which littered the floor. Soon silence reigned except for the sonorous snores of a burly ex-miner in the doorway. Almost before most of the men had dropped into a sound sleep a couple of men who had lost count of time and sense through a prolonged stay at the estaminet came rolling through the open door and fell sprawling over the sleeping inmates. Loud shouts, curses and confusion greeted this mode of entry and not a little scrapping took place until the sentry came to restore order by a timely warning of the night officer's approach. The two late ones continued to talk in a drunken undertone.

"Where's the bleedin' beer, mate?" "I've lost the bottle". "Clumsy sod" was the bitter retort. "You'd lose yer bloody 'ead yer would". "Awa wid ye and shut yere clap or I'll brain ye both" shouted a voice from the far end and the conversation died down and peace came to the barn.

Reveille came all too soon and sleepy inmates rubbed their eyes, lit candle ends and proceeded to take a wash outside in the trough that once had been used by horses. Then a scramble to pack kit, roll blankets for return to stores and breakfast was ready.

Do you, dear reader, want to thoroughly enjoy your breakfast? Then get up at 5am on a cold morning, wash in icy water and work for 20 minutes, then your bacon will taste delicious, your tea like nectar and your bread as succulent as hot rolls.

After breakfast companies were formed in the narrow country lanes; the united battalion was soon formed and, followed by the rumbling horse-drawn transport, started out for the unknown future wherein concerts, card parties, visits to estaminets, sports and all the little relaxations which had been indulged in, while resting and re-equipping, had no place. Instead we were to face hardship, extreme danger, and often hunger and death which would test to the uttermost the morale and esprit de corps of the Division.

The Royal Naval Division on arrival at its destination was attached to the 5th Army and soon some of the battalions took over a part of the line near Beaumont-Hamel and, the early October weather being unkind, our lot was not a happy one. Added to this discomfort came the news that General Paris, the old revered leader of the Division, was wounded while visiting the trenches[1]. This news was received as a bad omen. It was to

1. On 14 October 1916, Major General Sir Archibald Paris KCB was succeeded by General Shute

General Paris that most of the thanks were due for the independence and adherence to Naval code and pay that men of the Division enjoyed. Anyone outside the Division could not properly appreciate what a great thing it meant to the men to be controlled by the Admiralty, to hold naval ratings and also the great tradition which was an inspiration to all. Hence with General Paris out of the way, the officers and men feared they would be bound to the army and lose all the Naval privileges and ratings and all identity as a Naval Division - hence the sorrow and consternation.

After what seemed an unending time of trench digging, working parties, establishing dumps and all the work necessary in preparing for an attack, the Division was informed of its mission. This was to make a general attack on the German position, on the left bank of the river Ancre, between Beaumont-Hamel and Grandcourt.

The task was enormous as the enemy was well entrenched, with numerous strong points and forts which were to prove a great barrier to the advance of the British troops. Added to this the weather was becoming unsettled and persistent rain, mists and night frosts played havoc with the ground. As the previous onslaught in this district, undertaken in ideal circumstances, had not proved very successful, it was perhaps with a certain amount of misgiving that the Division entered the trenches. One great factor, which heartened all ranks, was the fact that they were to undertake this great task as an independent Division and not, as they feared, reinforced and submerged in the army.

18: Fury at Beaumont Hamel

The dull rumble of the guns, companies upon companies of men, more guns, some getting stuck in the mud, transport and still more men and guns wended their way by night to the scene of battle. Everyone was enveloped in thick misty rain, mud everywhere, curses, darkness lit only by the flash of guns. Returning from the Front were ambulances and hobbling men, empty limbers, pack horses bespattered with mud and tired men glad to be alive and going back for a brief respite. Such was the scene on a November night in 1916.

Bob and I were mere automatons, leg-weary, past feeling afraid, when we at last entered the trench from which we would shortly emerge to face the enemy's might. Men moved silently and ghost-like to their appointed battle positions and stood in thick mud and liquid water awaiting further commands.

"Got a fag, mate?" asked Bob's neighbours. "Yus, got a match?" and soon two red ends appeared and the sole comfort on such a night was indulged and enjoyed.

"Cigarettes out" whispered a voice and the next moment an officer appeared, whispered a few encouraging words and asked a few questions, then departed.

Soon our guns opened on the enemy lines and the enemy started replying. Pandemonium seemed to break loose. Everything from a rifle grenade to a howitzer contributed to the terrifying orchestra. Men's hearts were full of fear, yet they put a brave face on for the benefit of pals. Soon the order to "go over", and men moved across that death-acre immediately in front of them.

Out into the smoke and flash of bursting shells; shrieking, whining, thundering. It seemed impossible for even a rat to go safely across. Yet our boys, many young and new to all this, did succeed in reaching Jerry's front line; a skirmish, bombs thrown into dugouts, rifles fired, shrieks and curses, and soon a batch of prisoners were dashing across our trench line, glad to escape, if so they might, from this infernal hell. Some of the battalions had a nasty experience from concealed enemy machine guns and lost many men before taking their objective.

The thunders of guns increased in intensity, further batteries were rushed up to new positions, mud-caked horses gasped and panted, straining every muscle. Unhooked, they were rushed back for more ammunition. The roads, or mud tracks, leading to the battle area were packed with troops going up to succour their comrades, transport followed transport, and in the reverse direction came ambulances, stretchers, stricken men, bandaged but cheery - glad to get out of the inferno with only a wounded arm, leg or head. Many were the serious cases, shattered and bleeding; they presented a heart-rending sight in their muddy, blood stained khaki. Staff officers, transport officers and other officials of lower rank tried to keep some sort of order during these dark hours when gun flashes were the only light.

If Dante could have witnessed such a scene it would have given him ample matter for another "inferno"; in fact it seemed that a terrible monster lay not far away devouring the steady stream going forward and returning a few wrecks of his ferocity as evidence of his ghastly appetite.

Still the battle raged and through the long night hours our men were pressing forward, capturing a few trenches, gaining another strong point, killing and being killed in this frantic fight for a few fields, a shattered village and stream running red with blood. To those who still believe the enemy were cowards, let it be said that nothing could be further from the truth. They fought doggedly, giving ground slowly, holding on to their forts with untiring courage and tenacity and firing until the last bullet, the last man had been spent. English newspapers depicted the German as a coward, with arms in air, shouting "Kamerad". Some did surrender, and so did some of the men of the other armies; but mostly they presented a stern resistance, a proved and worthy foe. No need to wonder why the English advances appeared slow, the answer lay in the power of the enemy.

Many were the heroic deeds done during the continuous fighting in this area throughout November and it would fill many volumes to record only half of the heroism. Let it suffice to say that the Naval Division reached the final objective set for it, which included the village of Beaucourt - now a heap of battered masonry and broken homes. What tragedy to know that only a short time previously men had tilled those same fields where Death had now reaped his harvest. In that country church, now hardly recognisable, people, quiet, peace-loving, had worshipped every Sunday. Along those country lanes and paths down by the riverside, lovers had wandered in the cool of a summer evening. Where were those lovers now? Sadly one thinks of these things and of men's madness that makes a shambles of a garden. How will the river ever look the same again, with its weeping willows, its larch and fir trees, its oaks so proud - now lying prostrate, or shattered, or stark naked like accusing monuments to men's hatred.

And what was the price paid for this bit of stricken land lying about two miles north of the tragic town of Thiepval? Nearly 2,000 dead and nearly 3,000 wounded was the price for these one and a half square miles of mud and chaos. The glorious pride of this Division lay out in this land, while the hospital and dressing stations were filled, and only a wild-eyed handful of men from each battalion, hungry, tired, tried to breaking point, came away from this battlefield to take a couple of months' rest at, or near, Rue.

19: Resting at Rue then Jack returns

Gone were the sounds of guns, there remained only the quiet countryside, lowing of herds, rattle of country farm carts upon the roads, peace in the air, church bells ringing, buxom French women and pretty girls walking in the lanes, old men conversing in estaminets and at farm gates, workers in the fields and about the farm outbuildings. Yet, despite this Heaven after Hell, the men of the Naval Division could not appreciate it for some days, but walked about and did their duty in a mechanical way with eyes which still gazed vacantly, or held in them war's madness. Their souls and minds were still seared with dreadful nightmare memories.

I wandered, during off duty hours, among the lanes and byways trying to understand why I was left to face the future alone. Bob had "gone over the top" with me in that first advance and disappeared in a shell burst. Not a trace remained. In the heat and excitement I had not felt the loss of my chum as it seemed that he must somehow return, but away in the quiet of the countryside where the guns were not heard, except very faintly when the wind was in the right direction, I realised my loss. Bob Martyn had always been full of jest and good humour in a rough kind of way, his friends had always enjoyed his company and a great bond of friendship had been established. So on these December days all zest for soldiering had left me and I felt, like many others felt who had lost their best pals, distressed and low spirited.

A new draft was due to arrive and perhaps I would find one or two men I knew at the training camp at Blandford. I turned my steps in the direction of my billet, a fairly snug barn attached to a large farm just outside the town of Rue, and on arrival at the door found some newcomers were placing their kit in different parts, preparatory to falling in for tea rations.

Being dark inside I could not immediately discern their faces, but suddenly with a loud ejaculation one of the men came towards me.

"Fred Cornelius, by all that's wonderful".

"Jack Ferris in the flesh".

A silent hard hand grip followed and I now broke the spell of astonishment with "Well its great to see you again old man; all fit?"

"Yes thanks" answered Jack "and how is Bob?".

"Gone west".

"Poor chap, when?"

"Last affair, went over, shell burst, didn't see him again" came in broken, jerky words. I still felt Bob's death very keenly.

"What a cursed war this is, taking one at a moment's notice and always taking the best" murmured Jack.

Tea now broke up the conversation and later we went into the town and found a cheerful estaminet where we could get a table to ourselves and while away the evening with cards and conversation.

The reinforcements also began to drift into the estaminet and mingled with the others and soon games, drinks and music were in full swing. Also latest news was discussed, as men took up the threads of their meeting and recounted their experiences since that time. For the first time since early November, I began to feel a little less sad with the return of my pal Jack whom I did not expect to meet again, because men once recovered from wounds were often sent to an entirely different battalion.

Jack Ferris said how strained and pale I was; he knew instinctively what I, together with the divisional remnant, which occupied Rue, had suffered. Men's eyes showed what the soul and mind had suffered. No need for speech. Also the dearth of officers spoke volumes. We discussed briefly our experiences since we were parted at Bully Grenay and I congratulated Jack when he told me of the romance that was centred around a certain Ruth Carrington.

"Sounds funny" went on Jack "but where before I didn't fear the trenches, now I dread them, want to keep alive for her sake. If all husbands and fiancés feel like I do, they have my sympathy".

"Quite understand how you must feel" I replied. "If there wasn't a sweet girl I hope to win, I shouldn't care overmuch; in any case it doesn't seem right to be alive while so many decent, plucky chaps have gone just lately and are going west every day. Still, let's get off the topic and have a game."

"Yes, let's. What shall it be Fred - rummy?" "Aye".

66

So reunited, we forgot the war for a brief space and the estaminet resounded to chinks of glasses, rattle of cups, laughter and shouts of pleasure as the various games claimed our excited attention.

20: Horse transport in Howe Battalion

The days passed pleasantly doing light duties with just a little drill and marching thrown in to keep us fit. Men became familiar with the surrounding country and its inhabitants and many were the friendships fostered and cemented. Also new arrivals in the way of fresh troops constantly arrived to augment the Division's depleted ranks.

Came the month of January 1917 and, on a bright, frosty morning, preparations for a return visit to the "front" were put into full swing. Newly equipped, clean clothing, rifles, fresh ammunition, clean bodies and repaired health made the troops feel that it was still good to be alive. At practically full strength the Royal Naval Division left their rest camp and started on the long march back to the Ancre Valley to still further advance, only not against a confident enemy this time, but against an enemy who, through lack of rest and good food, was beginning to feel the strain and to lose some of their morale.

Much to my chagrin, I had been transferred to limberman in the Howe transport and thus severed for a time my newly regained friendship with Jack Ferris.

The Petty Officer in charge of this transport was tall, dark and fearless; he rode horses as though born to the saddle and was a charming fellow and well liked among most of the men. I immediately decided I liked him and would feel happy in my new job which consisted of applying the brake when necessary, cleaning the limber at the end of each day and assisting the driver, a Scot named Gordon, to load and unload and generally make my-self useful with the horses.

One day Gordon offered me a brief spell on the horses and I soon got the "feel" of them - a dark horse named "Sweep" and a brown and cream mare named "Maggie".

Promotion came quickly, for when the transport arrived at Engelbelmer I was given charge of a packhorse called "Titch", a quiet horse that suited a beginner. We quickly became pals and I felt proud of my horse, despite the caustic remarks of some of the other packhorse fellows regarding the thinness of Titch. Thin he was, but wiry and fit and could always be relied upon to do his duty and a bit more.

Throughout January and early February the ground was covered with snow and frost and proved a very trying time for men and beasts, especially as many additional duties were undertaken, moving food and ammunition dumps further up the riverbanks as the troops prepared to undertake a fresh advance. The horses became thinner and the poor creatures were unable to get full rations owing to the state of the frost-bound roads; also the stables in Engelbelmer consisted of nothing but the scanty shelter of shell-shattered cottages and barns, but despite this very little sickness was seen and the beasts, gallant creatures that they were, seemed to adopt the men's motto of "old soldiers never die, they only fade away".

The lot of our brave fellows in the trenches was even worse; shelter was scanty, duties were arduous and the activity of the artillery prevented long sleep. The advanced posts, or front line, were but a succession of shell holes, where men often froze to death for lack of movement and hot soup. Only at night could rations be conveyed to them and then often heavy gunfire would prevent them arriving, or relief from being effected. The only thing to long for was relief by fresh men but often that relief was too late. Imagine too a man, heavily laden with rations and ammunition, ploughing through thick mud in pitch darkness, looking for one particular shell hole where hundreds existed, and you will understand the difficulty of feeding and relieving the men in those advanced posts.

Jack Ferris was in a large dugout in reserve, but owing to continual working parties, night and day, he had in common with others little time in which to avail himself of its comparative comfort.

The medical officers had a busy time for there were hundreds of cases of frostbite to attend to in addition to the usual wounded cases, but no medical officer had a sinecure in France so they did not expect a soft time. In Engelbelmer, at one time a pleasant country townlet, transports were billeted in shell-shattered houses and barns and the men seldom undressed for sleep, except to unwrap putties and discard coats. The centre of amusement in the evening was the cook's galley, for there it was warm and with candles stuck on the wooden beams around the walls, men could indulge in their favourite games. Drink was scarce but most men had a fair supply of cigarettes, though of inferior brand.

On one such evening the Petty Officer strode in, called four packhorse drivers including me and, much loathe to leave, we departed for the stables to take our respective mounts up the line with a load of handbombs. The evening was bright starlight, the roads like glass and, after much slipping and sliding, we reached an advanced dump on the left bank of the Ancre. We loaded our ammunition on to the packsaddles and proceeded forward to the reserve trenches some half mile further up the river. Rae, a lean Scot, leading; me next; Brown, a Cockney and Dottle, a short good-humoured lad nicknamed "Dot", bringing up the rear. Silence reigned tonight over the battlefield for which we were thankful, especially as we were on a track that was well marked by enemy guns.

Four journeys were made and then the order was given for a return to home; simultaneously the guns opened out on either side in a grand strafe of hate. We were soon in the saddle and then began an exciting ride down the track, the horses at full stretch, jumping shell holes, slipping and sliding to the accompaniment of whizz-bangs and shrapnel. Rae, who was on Daisy, a mare of considerable speed, who later came into my charge as a real pal, easily outdistanced the others; suddenly to a blinding crash Titch fell and brought me headlong to the ground. The others, unaware, had carried on in this mad gallop to safety.

Quick as lightning, for a moment's delay may mean death, I was on my feet examining Titch and was glad to find him rising to his feet at my urging, but only a slow saunter would he go, despite the ear-splitting crashes and explosions around him. I felt very lonely at this moment with all my chums out of sight and with only a few men about, who were all taking what scanty shelter was available. With dry mouth and trembling limbs I led my faithful horse at a mere walk until the road was regained and the shelter of a ridge brought some measure of protection. "Thank God we're getting away from that lot Titch old boy" I confided to my horse "not healthy at all. What's up now old boy, can't you get along?" For Titch had again sunk to his knees and was gasping. He made another gallant effort and proceeded about 400 yards further when he collapsed and rolled over on his side, panting heavily. I was full of solicitude and concern, knelt down and patted his soft nose and whispered encouragement, but faithful Titch had walked his last and was entirely exhausted. The wind was keen and the night was bitterly cold so I looked around for cover and found some sandbags with which I could cover my pal, and I also placed some under his head. I decided to stay by my horse, despite the deserted road and little hope of help, so I lit a cigarette, sat down beside Titch and patted his nose and comforted the poor beast whose life was rapidly ebbing, the best I could. "Poor Titch, why need you die old boy?" "It's not your fault this cursed war" I whispered in a choked voice "try and live old chum, I'm fond of you".

Hours went by and still Titch lay gasping; sore at heart and nearly frozen beyond feeling I remained by his side. About 3am the gallop of horses' hooves sounded in the distance and soon the Petty Officer arrived with a spare horse. As I had not returned with the others, it was assumed that I had been wounded or had lost my horse, hence the action of the Petty Officer bringing along a spare horse. One look at Titch and the kindly PO decided to put him immediately out of his misery. He knelt beside him, patted him, murmured "poor old boy" and with his revolver shot him through the head. With a quick quiver Titch lay dead and we pulled him to the side of the road for later burial. So one poor faithful "friend of man" passed into the animals' heaven having given good and true service to his masters, and both of us who witnessed his passing felt sad and could not speak for a few minutes. The Petty Officer broke the silence by offering his water bottle to me saying "Have a sip of rum old man, you must be frozen". I took several good sips and returned the bottle with thanks; now that the strain was over I felt suddenly cold and tired. The night ride across snow-covered tracks and fields to Engelbelmer brought some little warmth to my body and after a meal round the cook's fire I dropped into a sound slumber. Next morning I was given charge of Daisy, the pretty mare, and she certainly was a consolation. So knowing, cute and lovable, that she soon won away any man's heart.

Days passed and another attack was made on the German position on both sides of the Ancre, more ground was gained, more men lost their lives, more casualties sent to hospital. Fighting day after day the Germans were being surely pressed further and further back. Jack Ferris, sick at heart sometimes, yet sticking to his job like so many others, still found time to smile and to dare think of what a few years might bring. He had

1. Over 480,000 horses and pack mules were killed or died serving the British forces in the war and more transport was drawn by horses than by vehicles.

been in the thick of the fighting several times and had come through unharmed in body, but with mind seared with ghastly sights and sounds.

I, like many others, had thought a transport job was "cushy" but I found it decidedly arduous and dangerous in the extreme. No trenches or dugouts, or even shell holes to shelter in, but just a mad, heart-throbbing dash into the danger area each evening, with heavy artillery playing on the roads and fields, and a quick unload and a gallop back. Sometimes when wagons were hit, the road blocked with wreckage, a wait of 10, 20 or even 30 minutes would ensue, when men, horses and wagons would have to wait patiently on the road, while death came very near. No shelter at all, only a hope that the shelling would cease or would shift to other areas. For cool nerve and cold-blooded pluck I commend a driver quietly sitting on his horse awaiting further commands, while the earth is being rent all around and lead rain descends from the sky. If you ducked down against your horse's neck they probably took fright because fear is quickly communicated from man to beast; horses that took fright could wreak great havoc so it was best to sit still.

Transport men also saw more of the havoc of war, for after a fresh offensive they often had to pass along a road or track where dead Germans and English laid sprawled with glazed eyes and bleached faces upturned to the skies. Here a young German, no older than 18 years, lay with an unexploded grenade in his clenched hand, another lying near as if in sleep, while a young English boy with fair hair appeared to be sitting resting awhile at the side of the road, yet his eyes fixed in their glassy stare told the truth. Yet again other English and Germans had, apparently, crawled close to each other when death was near in order to have some little human contact when life was ending; for the close embrace seemed to indicate a brotherly feeling for each other when horrible wounds made them afraid of loneliness. Strange, yet not so strange after all, that men forgot their hatred when about to make the "great adventure". Human sympathy is God-like and outlasts all petty hatreds, jealousies and greed; and it is good to know that the men found an antidote, when in pain, to all the strife which politicians would make. While MPs at home in every land breathed hatred and babbled of patriotism, and hid behind them the horrors of war, the men who did the job were first to forgive when strife ceased for a while, and the prisoners taken were found to be quite human and likeable - not the fierce, inhuman, degraded beasts one was led to imagine by the descriptions given to the enemy by newspapers and public men in high authority. Some of the enemy were beasts, insofar that war gave them the right to do atrocious things such as raping, looting and killing of little children, but these beings exist in every nation and army and, anyway, why blame them entirely. War wreaked havoc with men's souls and women's bodies and made them commit themselves to vile things, which, in a saner moment, would horrify them.

21: Out of the line, near Arras

The war rolled on. The English had made several huge bites in the German main defence lines and had, to put it in soldiers' parlance, "Got Jerry on the run" in several areas. The French were also once again taking the offensive and the people in the allied countries were fed daily with the prospect of more victories to come so that, to them, a new optimism was coming to relieve the depression which had fallen upon them during the previous year.

At the battle front it seemed harder to believe that peace would ever come, as with each fragment of land regained so many good men were slain that, when one stopped to consider the cost of pushing the enemy out of France, the brain would reel and a fatalistic attitude would make men doubt if peace would ever come to stricken Europe.

The Royal Naval Division, having accomplished its mission on the Ancre, was withdrawn from this battle zone and marched with rising spirits to Hedauville, thence to trek forward to Busnes, near Arras, where they had to rest and recondition for a coming fresh trial of strength with the enemy. However, the brief return to civilisation and decent ways of living did much to restore men who had become mere automatons with war-weary faces and drooping shoulders. The divisional bands were again in evidence and helped to restore the flagging spirits of the troops. To witness the joy among the men, by the receipt of fresh boots and clean clothing, would leave most civilians cold; but to those who for two months had washed in dirty shell-hole water, worn badly-washed clothes, cleaned mud-caked khaki tunics and putties, only to become saturated again in a few hours, suffered from vermin until every inch of the body itched, this change of clothing, good clean baths and clean tunics came as a joy and a tonic. Nothing like being clean to restore happiness and good morale.

What a change to behold, towns and villages almost untouched by war's ravages; to see French womenfolk again, to watch the old menfolk busy about the farms and cottages when only a few days previously the endless desolation and smashed villages of Ancre valley were the only views to greet the eyes. Two months of this desolation would drive most men to despair, so that the sight of a pretty French village unscathed, and of coy French girls, produced a joy out of all proportion to the surroundings. To exchange badinage in the little village shops where eggs, bread, coffee and chocolates could be obtained, as well as a lot of trinkets for the folks at home, was another delight indulged. All this may sound feeble to some but, when one had come back from a bleak desert of mud, ice and destruction, the very simple things of life appealed with irresistible force and brought smiles to drawn faces, sanity to seared minds and a belief in the good God above.

I met Jack Ferris again and, together with other chums, we were waking the echoes in an old farm building with songs and jests.

"Good to sing again, 'eh Mate?" observed one of their number.

"Yes, rather old boy; how about another drop of 'vin blong'?"

The wine bottle went from lips to lips until empty and then a little game of cards, followed by more singing. Ribald songs they were, but they relieved the strain and caused nerves over-taut to relax. More jokes, mostly of a doubtful character, followed; but they brought laughter to make these boys forget sorrow.

"Now Lofty, you tell one". Thus addressed, I began:

"Two tarts were walking along Brighton front when ......" A low tap at the door cut short the story and the Padre walked in, with a cheery yet sad smile, to chat awhile with the men and to lead thoughts to a higher plane. Then he told some good jokes, clean and witty, which caused much merriment and earned him the name of "good sort". He was held in high esteem for he did not funk when danger was around the corner and it nearly always was.

"Having a service next Sunday, Padre?" asked one. "I hope so" he replied "but if possible don't forget worship comes from the heart and need not wait for a service to commence.

Well boys, goodnight and God bless you" and so he left.

"Good sort that chap, lives good and acts good and doesn't spout too much" remarked Jack Ferris and his opinion was endorsed by all. So one good man lived the Christ-like life in adverse circumstances and would there were more like him.

During this quiet period of rest the letter and parcel mails were delivered more regularly and, of course, Jack Ferris always had a letter from Ruth who, though anxious for the sake of her lover, bravely went about her numerous duties and comforted and cheered many a weary wounded warrior. These letters he treasured, as lovers do, and only the general news therein would he read to me and I, in return, would laughingly accuse him of deception.

"What a fat packet for you this time Jack".

"Yes, like to hear about her Fred?"

"Carry on Jack".

The letter was read, or at least parts of it, and at the finish I would remark "What an interesting letter".

"Jealous, Fred?"

"No, only critical, doesn't mention a word of love" I bantered.

"Go to hell" laughed Jack "and find a maid to write love letters to you".

"Not to hell, Jack old bean, only Etaples".

"You wouldn't stand an earthly with Ruth".

"Rot Jack, I would soon capture your sweetheart's fancy".

"Well, you'd have to alter your face a bit Corny, old boy, she prefers them handsome".

"Alright, you win" I smiled "get the cards and we'll do something useful instead; but if I ever get to Etaples, I'll say goodbye to Ruth on your account. Oh! You blighter" for a well-aimed pack of cards caught me on the nose. After that came peace and a game until "lights out".

22: The battle for Gavrelle

The early dawn of 9 April found the various units of the Naval Division marching into the firing line once again; that morning was very quiet. It was a typical spring morning with nature trying its best to heal the scars of men's destruction in the trees and bushes and fields. Everywhere buds were bursting, fresh grass peeping slyly out of the earth, as if half afraid to venture forward, and early spring flowers were raising brave faces to the sky. Even the birds were songfully employed and it seemed strange to hear their notes so close to the trenches, where death and destruction might reign supreme within the next hour. More than a few thoughts of English lanes and countryside were present in men's minds as they wended their way to and from the battlefields on this early spring morning. Easter holidays, and all they mean to the workers of a nation, seemed very far away and not even the most hardened warrior could help feeling a little "fed up" when realising what might have been if war had not come to Europe.

The position of affairs in general at this time was as follows: on the eastern front the Russians were being driven back; the French were attempting a big advance which did not meet with the desired success; and the British were taking the offensive to aid the French, by making the Germans keep a large number of men in reserve to meet the British onslaught. The enemy was still very strong in men and materials and the position on the eastern front allowed the Germans to take away some number of divisions for use on the western battlegrounds, so our troops found a very determined resistance to their efforts to advance.

An endeavour was being made to capture the whole of Vimy Ridge to enable an advance to take place in the Arras region. Only a partial success greeted their efforts so that during the next few days the Royal Naval Division had a gruelling time in their attack on Gavrelle, a one-time pleasant country village, now like a miniature fort, for its cellars were machine gun nests and on either side of the village was a veritable maze of trenches and machine gun posts, strong points and barbed wire. Commander Asquith distinguished himself in the taking of this village, for by the time our boys had partly accomplished their task, so many had been killed and wounded and so few officers were left that the situation would have become very serious if the scattered parties, in occupation of the main village, were not immediately united and led forward to complete their work.

This was a most hazardous task, but Commander Asquith rallied the tired men, instituted some order, and prepared to lead them forward to the final objective. A large manor house, which formed a German fort, was likely to cause a serious stumbling block to our advance but this the gallant Commander soon turned into an English fort by capturing the Germans inside it, with the aid of a small party, and placing a Lewis gun crew[1] to keep watch and hold up any enemy counter attack.

By this time, the situation in Gavrelle was desperate. Artillery from both sides pounded the houses into dust and brick heaps, not even the cellars were safe, and the men in occupation were being blown to atoms during every minute of the delayed advance. Thirsty, worn out and hungry these gallant boys yet rallied to the call for further advance and soon the whole village, and a little beyond, was in our possession. The situation however was still serious for, owing to the failure of some troops on the left of the village, the remnants of the Drake and Hood battalions found their flank exposed and it needed only a strong German counter attack to cause confusion and disaster to our troops holding the village. For that reason, the Lewis gun crew emerged from the Manor House and engaged the enemy hotly, with rapid fire, until the whole crew were killed or mortally wounded[2]. For this gallant sacrifice the Division had to be extremely thankful because it probably saved hundreds from annihilation by delaying an enemy counter attack.

1. *Douglas Jerrold records that this party was led by Sub-Lieutenant Cooke RNVR Brigade Intelligence*
2. *Douglas Jerrold records that there was one survivor: Leading Seaman Charlton who was awarded the DCM.*

78

During the remainder of the day numerous bodies of men rejoined their battalions, having been separated in the confusion of the advance; a general sorting out took place and measures were taken to consolidate our gains. The night was dark and quiet, almost as if mourning the dead who lay about on barbed wire, in shell holes, along the village streets and huddled in all sorts of fantastic attitudes among the ruined houses. What frightful waste. This rotting flesh, which only a few hours previously had talked, joked, enjoyed (as far as possible) life in the trenches and had breath and pulsating veins. The living dared not think of the day's carnage for fear of losing their reason. What a merciful thing that they were physically and mentally exhausted, it prevented thought.

Relief by troops which had been in reserve was carried out during the night and, early next morning, frightened, war-stained Germans, crawled out of hiding from the cellars and underground passages of the houses in Gavrelle and surrendered. Poor creatures, one felt sorry for them, mere boys in their 'teens who needed sympathy. That is the curse of war; it catches in its terrible grip the boys of a nation and turns them into maniacs, cowards or devils, according to its effect on different natures.

Guards were placed around the prisoners, they were marched to the rear and kind hearted Tommies offered them cigarettes, water and a few dry biscuits, which brought grateful looks to the faces of those boys who throughout the previous day had faced the fury of the British guns.

The great lesson one learned in the war was that, in a general way, hatred of the enemy was only indulged by men and women who never witness war, while pity and sympathy was displayed only by the contestants. Exceptions there were, but one saw more hatred in England than ever one witnessed among our fellows at the front. Strange, but true.

23: Daylight transport mission near Arras

What happened to me during these momentous days?

I had shared bivouac with a Devonshire lad, big-limbed, slow of speech, rugged complexion with a good nature that was very attractive. The transport column had pitched camp on the heights overlooking Arras and near Roclincourt, a small village with only a few houses intact. Nevertheless, good use was made of this village as a dump for ammunition, cattle fodder and food for the troops. Roclincourt lay about 3 miles behind the front line and, therefore, was often shelled by the enemy; hence the transport lines and troops in reserve occupied bivouacs and tents on the neighbouring slopes. In this sector of the line, the transport had a "hot time" for the roads leading to the battlefields were well marked by enemy artillery.

The first occasion on which rations were taken up the line by the Howe transport occurred on a warm sunlit day and, not suspecting the hazardous mission before them, the men were in high spirits for it appeared that in this sector no night journeys would be needed. What a surprise awaited them!

No limbers were taken on this first journey, only packhorses, and after loading the saddles the journey started. I brought up the rear with a big black mule that seemed to know what he wanted and intended to get his way. The journey had not long commenced before this big creature, about $16^{1}/_{2}$ hands high, started to jib and make determined efforts to return to camp. Firm handling kept him in the right direction for some time and he followed the front horses, docilely, until the cavalcade reached the Arras -

Gavrelle road when a sudden determined jerk of the head wrenched the reins from my hands and away trotted the mule in the direction of camp.

I shouted to the others in front and they turned back to chase my stubborn pal who, with an amazing manner common to mules, just kept a distance of about 20 yards ahead. As I quickened my pace so he would speed up a bit, apparently quite content to do enough and no more to evade capture.

After a mile of this freedom the mule suddenly stopped, perhaps loneliness, or the consciousness that he was playing coward, or again his pity for me, caused him to stop and wait his capture. Breathless and in a rage, I caught his rein and gave him a piece of my mind which quite failed to disturb the benign look on the mule's face. Perhaps my black friend had learned similar language from other men and, in consequence, accepted the insults with good grace. By this time the other members of the transport were well out of sight and I had to proceed in the direction they had gone but with not the slightest idea of where to go after reaching the crest of the hill overlooking Gavrelle.

So the two of us, still distrustful of each other, made progress to the hillcrest and there met the others returning from the unknown. And what a sight met our eyes. Three of the drivers bandaged, all of them perspiring and looking ghastly, and two horses missing.

"Where do I go?" I asked the first one.

"Down this bleeding road to Hell" was a comment and "Goodbye Corny boy, I'll draw your pay tomorrow".

"Bad as that?" I asked.

"Yes, and worse" remarked another "sorry you haven't got a pal to go with, but the Petty Officer is waiting for you at the dump by the roadside, and he says "hurry Cornelius up, or he'll find a corpse".

"Thanks" I replied, then another word or two with the others and I turned to my mule with the comment "Come on you old black devil, we're in for it and no mistake. Cheerio boys".

"Rough luck going alone ain't it?" said Cookson, a kind-hearted Cockney lad "bad enough with pals, but damn rotten on your own with a bloody obstinate mule".

"Yes" commented others, and they proceeded to camp, glad to escape so lightly from the Hell just the other side of the hill. Somehow it was always like that up here, death always waited for you "just over hill" or "round the corner". It always came at unexpected times and places. A lovely ravine, slightly war-scarred, would be very peaceful at 3pm on a summer afternoon but at 3.05pm it would be pandemonium, and death called.

I and my mule faced the task ahead with no small amount of fear. The road before us was well marked with shell holes, here and there lay dead horses and mules and further on lay dead men propped up against the earth walls either side of the road.

These stared at me with unseeing eyes, and on some faces was hatred, some fear, some a ghastly smile. It was horrible! I did not wonder why my pals returned sweating from such scenes.

The gunfire was increasing in intensity and some shells were "finding" the road. A group of stretcher-bearers taking shelter in a "funk hole" called to me, but the noise of the guns prevented me from hearing them. I dared not stop to listen for only iron determination was driving me to walk down that road to worse scenes of destruction. In fact I became almost detached in mind, wondered how soon death would come, thinking of my folks at home, looking at my mule to see that he was breathing heavily through fright but quite unhurt. A prayer escaped my lips asking God for safety for my mule and myself, I felt calmer now, almost unafraid.

Shrapnel continued to burst overhead and pattered on the road all around. I looked towards Gavrelle, in the valley, which was a smoking mass of ruins. On the fields all around great gaps appeared, miniature earthquakes. The noise was terrific, stunning, deafening. On we walked and I crept closer to my mule, patted him and spoke to him. The beast looked at me in a questioning way as if trying to ask why he was being brought into this inferno. I gave him another friendly pat, it was good to feel that I had a living friend in this road of death. Fear brought man and beast very near together on this lone journey.

On we went until it seemed that we must walk right into the enemy lines, just beyond Gavrelle, when quite suddenly the Petty Officer hailed us from the roadside. I almost ran the last few yards - what a relief to know the journey was ended. No time for explanations, but a quick unloading of saddle, a shouted word or two between us and then I said "Coming back now Petty Officer?".

"No Cornelius, must wait here until the trench working party arrives; but you get back out of this hell as quick as you can".

"Right ho PO!, I'll get" I shouted, trying to make my voice heard above the guns.

Much as I would have liked company on the homeward journey, I felt less afraid now that I was turning my back on the scene and, with a shout to my mule, we started back at a trot. Spent shrapnel hit my helmet, bits of earth flew into the road, but somehow we escaped injury.

We were nearing the crest of the hill, the other side of which meant comparative safety, when Mr. Mule decided, quite definitely, to stop - and no inducement would make him move. Praise, argument, force, all failed and I almost felt like leaving him and getting away when suddenly, above the general thunder of the guns, a terrific shriek sounded and three great shells burst on the hill crest right in the road. I fell flat on my face, the mule quivered and next moment started to trot forward up the hill. I tore after him and caught him up on the hilltop where we had to go round the three great new gaps made in the road.

"Phew Nigger, what an escape" I gasped when I recovered breath. "Thanks old pal for stopping when you did else we should not be alive now. Clever beggar, you must have smelt those coming". Nigger simply flapped an ear in acknowledgement of the compliment, looked wisely at me, then set his face steadily in the direction of camp and kept up a steady slouching walk until he arrived there.

"Here's Cornelius" called Cookson to some pals inside their tent "looks pretty done up too. Well Corny had an enjoyable afternoon walk?".

"Good Lord, Cookie, what a hotspot and what damn madness to take us up that road in broad daylight. Jerry must have seen us quite plainly walking down the road".

"Yes mate I bet he did, but soldiers are cheap so why need the officers worry; all the same I can't understand them allowing horses to take the risk, they cost money, we don't!".

A welcome dixie of tea came out of the cookhouse and everyone became too busy to talk. Strong tea, thick bread and butter and Australian jam are very great luxuries to men who only a short 30 minutes ago had not expected to eat another tea.

Someone had blundered when ordering that daylight trip to Gavrelle, for all future excursions up the line were taken by night.

24: Night-time happenings

One night the drivers were all tucked up in their tents asleep, preparing for a strenuous morrow, when an ear-splitting explosion rent the air wakening, with starts and thudding hearts, the occupants of the tents.

"What the hell was that?" nervously asked one of the number.

"Oh! One of the horses blew off I expect!" came the answer from another quarter of the tent.

No one moved for a second or two and then the Petty Officer popped his head into tent flap and shouted "Jerry's hit an "ammo" dump in Roclincourt, but don't get wind up and don't strike matches. Stand by for orders; we may have to move if he gets the range of our camp".

"Right ho!" came in chorus and soon tunics were on and we waited outside the tent watching the blazing dump down in the valley. No further shelling took place and soon came the order to get back to bed.

Another night, it was always nighttime when things happened, several enemy planes bombed the Arras road and surrounding camps and the transport received a full share of the excitement. The poor horses were terrified as bits of spent shrapnel fell among them and the men had the utmost difficulty in restraining them and soothing them.

The traffic policeman on duty at the junction of the Arras-Roclincourt road was blown to atoms and many men and horses were wounded. These night affairs always caused a certain amount of panic for no-one had the slightest idea where the planes were until the bombs dropped and there was not the slightest form of cover, except here and there, a dilapidated dugout where half a dozen men might hide and, even then, the vibration brought down steady streams of dirt from the roof on to the occupants.

Picquet duty at night in the horse lines was an eerie experience. The horizon all around was constantly lit up by gun flashes and shell bursts, throwing into relief the shattered buildings and stark leaf-stripped trees. Dark shadows of men moved across the fields to their various destinations, either going to the line or returning from it, and transport could be heard bumping and rattling along the distant cobbled roads.

The eternal rise and fall of flare lights added to the mystery and the droning of the planes on night patrol reminded one of dragon flies or of giant mosquitoes on a summer evening. Occasionally, a white ghost-like car would pass along the main road to Arras and one knew that more battered wrecks were leaving the zone of Hell.

25: Rest at Roclincourt before fierce fighting

On a typical spring day at the end of April, the Division was relieved and went back, for a brief rest, to the slopes surrounding Roclincourt. The casualties numbered about 4,000 officers and men so the Division, sadly depleted, was to be reinforced by fresh men. How often during this death struggle did Divisions of strong young men, full of the pride and healthy vigour of English manhood, return from the "line" or battleground broken and battered to have a "breather" for a few days? Many hundreds of times this occurred during the war and one sickened at times with all the wastage of gallant men, known to their loved ones as sweethearts, brothers, husbands and fathers. How many thousands have no graves but are lying in small pieces of muscle and bone and flesh all over the battlefields of the worldwide war? Smashed men, devastated land, bereft homes, enormous national debts, are the fruits of conflict, and yet one hears and reads of men (or are they fools?) upholding war as a purifier of nations.

Courage, sacrifice and devotion to duty are in evidence, but so also is cowardice, selfishness, bestiality and immorality. So why exalt war? Mankind produces just the same virtues and vices in peace, so why the feeble argument of war being a purifier?

Perhaps the next international disagreement will be settled by the leaders of every nation settling it among themselves; it would certainly not bring in any innocent people, or wipe out the best of a nation's manhood, while still leaving the vipers and warmongers safe and alive.

The rest at Roclincourt did wonders for the men and, although various working parties and "fatigues" were wanted, the time available for relaxation and recreation was quite sufficient to allow the men to forget war for a time, despite the proximity of the guns, and to pay visits to Arras, the YMCA concerts and other interesting places - so time passed pleasantly.

Jack Ferris and I saw quite a lot of each other during these early May days and in leisure hours repaired to concerts or games huts and spent many a pleasant hour. Also, nearly each mail contained letters or parcels from home and we always eagerly awaited the arrival of the mail limber that brought the mailbags from a distant railhead. Our chief delight was, of course, in receiving letters from Ruth Carrington and Florence Allen and, although we shared most things together, we always chaffingly refused to allow each other the privilege of reading these particular letters.

"We spend half our pay in notepaper" I remarked on one occasion "but it's a good investment".

"Aye aye" replied Jack "what's life in the 'land navy' without a girl to write to?"

"Damn rotten Jack".

"Still Fred, we have nothing to grumble about, haven't been killed yet, like poor old Bob".

"Fancy that being a thing to be glad about, that you're alive; wouldn't it sound funny in peacetime?".

"Yes Fred old man it would. And yet no chap knows how good it is to be alive until he has been facing up to death or glory, mostly death with just a spot of glory. It's a rum kind of existence and yet I wouldn't be a "conchy" for all the money in the world. How could you face the folk at home knowing you had funked it?

"No Jack, I shouldn't have the nerve, I should feel a worm".

"What about a bit of letter writing" reminded Jack.

"Passed unanimously old man".

Silence reigned whilst pencils scrawled and as we sat on upturned beer cases we confided our thoughts to paper.

The activities on this Arras front now became subdued and only one or two fierce enemy charges were dealt with. Otherwise it was simply trench warfare, with all its monotony and general sapping of strength, without the excitement and danger of advance. The Division was alternately working behind the lines, helping to make strongholds in reserve and taking its share of the trench routine.

Wandering one afternoon in late May, I found myself in one of the old battlefields, now deserted, except for the birds that inhabited the sprouting bushes. The grass had fully covered the collapsed walls of the trenches as if to hide from men the scenes of bitterness and strife, the evidence of brutality. No trace remained of shell holes, they were now only undulations in the carpet of grass. "Wonderful how nature repairs the damage" I thought "God's handiwork again".

I wandered on for some distance admiring the Union Jack colours on the ground provided by red poppies, blue cornflowers and white anemones and truly it made a pretty picture; only the distant growl of guns and rumbles of war vehicles, and the knowledge that hundreds of dead men lay beneath this beauty of nature, prevented me from feeling absolutely happy.

Several more of my comrades in the transport were coming along the road so I joined them and together we returned to the camp, singing as we walked.

Jack Ferris was on work detail in the reserve so had little time for admiring the countryside. In fact, where he worked only the drear shell-marked earth was on view and in the distance, down in a hollow, lay the ruin of Gavrelle. The sunlight glinted on the white washed walls still standing and every few seconds a puff of smoke would appear over the village, or a cloud of dust would rise from the ruins, and one knew that the Germans were still pounding the wrecked homes of a one-time happy little community.

May, the month of beauty to people living in the country unharmed, passed away leaving only greater dreariness in this war zone and June entered to find the earth desolate. The night of June 8, which happened to be my 21st birthday, nearly proved my last, for the transport went up with food and ammunition and just when approaching a ridge, which formed part of the support line of trenches, German artillery opened out and for the next five minutes (it seemed years) pandemonium reigned.

The first three shells dropped with a crash to the rear of the horses and four of them stampeded. One packhorse was badly wounded and one driver hit. Everyone was deafened and suffering from concussion and I, who had now become leader of the line, could only see the officer in charge gesticulating; automatically, like one in a dream, I got to my feet again and led the way forward. My horse, by the name of Sweep, was unhurt and seemed to keep cool in this trying time and almost led me along to the dumping ground. The others followed and the next salvo of shells burst, two drivers slightly wounded and one horse broke away. The trench working party soon had the survivors unloaded and doubtless rations were scanty that night in the trenches. Only a few shells, but it meant short fare and hungry stomachs for hundreds of men; such is the thin thread that connects the front line with civilisation.

I was the first man away and the officer shouted "Go past the ridge at the gallop if you want to reach camp tonight" and not needing a second bidding, I mounted into the empty pack saddle and put old Sweep to a clattering, clumsy gallop. If you could have seen that old hairy limber horse move you would have backed him, shirt and all, for the next Derby.

I got safely past the ridge and out into the open and then pulled Sweep to a standstill to await the others. Jerry still persisted in his shelling but, awaiting their opportunity, the whole party, or rather what remained, came safely into the open track which led to the main Arras road.

By this time the guns all along the line were indulging in a strafe of hate and only by shouting to each other could the drivers make themselves heard. I found out that my bedmate was badly hurt and left in the charge of some ambulancemen. Another pal, by the name of Dottle, was found to be unaccounted for, so I and another man waited behind to eventually find Dottle staggering along alone, minus his horses, and in a very dazed, deafened state. We promptly took him between us and assisted him home, and after two days off duty he felt fit again.

"A rotten night's work Bill" I commented "three drivers wounded, several horses lost and the troops short of ammo and grub". Bill grunted assent. No need to talk, it was only just a small, every night, occurrence among the transports of the line, but important enough when a good pal was hurt and perhaps dead.

Up in the line itself matters were very grave for the advanced positions were practically cut off by a heavy enemy barrage. Men were crouching on the broken firestep wondering when their turn would come. The shriek of small shells, whine of shrapnel and whizzbangs, which came to one so suddenly, were playing havoc with nerves already tired and stretched to breaking point. Some of the new recruits had the look of madness in their eyes and it required only one to lose control of himself, to influence others and cause a stampede. Still the pitiless barrage went on, our guns replying strenuously, and officers and non-commissioned officers walked along the battered trenches trying to encourage the men in their charge by steeling themselves to making casual comments on the heavy fire, joking sometimes, and offering a cigarette to different men who seemed on the verge of collapse.

All night the terrifying thunder, heaving earth and rocking dugouts, shattered eardrums and numbed the senses. Men who had faced many similar bombardments did their best to keep the youngsters steady, but it was a hard task with reminders of death so constantly facing them.

A man, watching over the parapet, would suddenly fall back with the top half of his head blown off; another would collapse with a bullet through the brain, another with stomach gaping after a gash made by flying shell fragment, still another with gaping neck wounds, and so on along the whole trench. The shrieks of agony, curses, groans adding to the general horror of the situation.

One becomes mentally dead, or goes raving mad, or sobs for home in such circumstances. Thoughts cease to be as men wait for the end. How hopeless to pit physical strength and mental alertness against such powers. One can do nothing, nothing at all, until the barrage lifts and then the nerve-taut survivors fire away, for very life itself, into the great moving mass of enemy troops pouring towards the thinly held line. Machine guns spit, rifles snap, bombs are flung and the grey masses get thinner. Still they come on, nearer ever nearer, dropping for a breather, rising to dash forward again and, when the small defending remnant seemed to be almost doomed to destruction, a terrific fire opens from the British guns, crashing, crushing, smashing to pulp the advance.

Suddenly, shouts from the rear and fresh English boys are coming to the relief and, jumping the front trench, complete the work of the guns and drive the Germans back to their trenches.

Another attack failed; hundreds of dead and dying lie in No Man's Land and their cries are heard all throughout the following day and night. Some are brought in at night but few survive. One man goes raving mad and runs over the top to destruction, others collapse now the strain is temporarily over, and others resort to coarse jokes, sleep or cursing. Anything, no matter how trivial, so long as it keeps them sane and alive. The simplest, silliest things become of great account and men laugh (the anguished laugh) to break the strain and to stop serious thought.

The one important day finally comes, the day when relief troops arrive. In the early morning the advance party arrives quickly followed by the main body. Dugouts, war stock and latest news are handed over to the relieving companies. Position of enemy trenches, its strength and all the facts of interest to the incoming troops are discussed. Let the two different sources of information speak for themselves. The men exchange positions in the trenches.

"'Ere you are mate, see that ruddy 'ouse on the right, well, that's Jerry's strong point and 'is line runs from there to there".

"Bloody 'ot its been lately too".

"Say, kid, we'll show 'em wot war is" says a new arrival.

"No need to worry old son, the bleedin 'un will show you first. Anyways you are welcome and think of me 'anging round the canteen tonight" retorts the relieved one. "Oh, and by the way, count them Mills' bombs, should be forty 'free all told". "Cheerio Cock and best of luck".

The officers hand over details in the dugout.

"Morning Captain A, what a jolly rough time you had yesterday, heard about it at the Headquarters".

"Yes, just 42 men and two COs, one Second Lieutenant and myself left".

"Good God, is that all?"

"Yes, old man, we don't need much relieving; anyhow let's exchange news".

The next ten minutes was spent in giving and receiving detailed information of enemy strength, positions, guns, strong points etc. and how much available ammunition, good dugouts, state of trenches and general news of our position on either flank.

"Looks rather serious A, not much depth or solidity in our position, but still I have good fresh men in my company".

"That's a very important point. Hope you have a decent time and not too many rats to supper".

"Got any whisky old man?"

"Yes, have a drink" and producing the bottle they both fill cracked cups and drink to each other's health.

"Cheerio and best of luck".

"Thanks and au revoir".

Always, officers and men exchange these words "best of luck" and it seemed to be the countersign to bring safety to the one going into a dangerous job. Men and women saying it to their boys and, parting from them at the railway stations, would echo the same words as a prayer, "best of luck John and do be careful". It rang through England, it was taken up in France, and instead of "goodbye" it became "good luck".

As care and foresight and skill could not combat the death aimed at one from five to ten miles away by an unseen enemy, so "luck" was called in by everyone to keep them from harm. Deep down in men's hearts luck perhaps stood for something far deeper than mere chance, only they called everything either lucky or unlucky. For instance, to escape a serious strafe unhurt was sometimes lucky or unlucky according to a man's frame of mind. If a small 'Blighty' wound was received it was lucky and many men were openly and unashamedly wishing for a wound that would take them back to England for a while. One would often hear the remark from a man who had seen lengthy active service that he had been unlucky not to have had a 'Blighty' one. This was the reasoning put into a proposition:

Small wound in leg or elsewhere	=	4 to 6 weeks at rear of battle area, with a chance of getting to England
No wound	=	Carry on fighting
Carry on with the fighting	=	i. Tired to exhaustion and nerve-racked OR ii. Serious wound OR iii. Blown to atoms

Can you wonder that a 'Blighty' wound was considered lucky?

26: Shelling

Standing outside my tent one evening, looking away to Arras in the distance, I suddenly became aware of a new and rather sinister gunfire.

"What's that Bill?" I asked an occupant of the tent.

"Don't know Lofty, sounds like a big Jerry gun" replied Bill, at the same time emerging from the tent with a lousy shirt in his hand.

"There's the sound again".

"Ye Gods and that shell landed in Arras".

"Where?"

"Nine o'clock of our field kitchen, there - see that smoke, and there goes another".

A rending of the upper air, a crash and blinding flash revealed the destination to be Arras Cathedral, or near that building.

"So Jerry can reach Arras 'eh Bill?"

"Yes he can, no safety anywhere now Lofty, and what price those women in Arras; they won't 'arf get the wind up".

The shells continued to fall on Arras for half an hour and then came silence, but it's a nasty shock to know the enemy can reach an objective 20 miles away.

"If they can get to Calais, they'll be having a pop at Dover" ruminated Bill.

"Quite likely".

"More wind up in Blighty!"

"Expect Jerry will be mighty glad to get to Calais 'eh Bill?".

"Yes, and so should I for a clean shirt and a kiss from a pretty girl".

"Harry and Nigger went to Arras tonight".

"Did they Lofty?"

"Yep".

"After the birds I suppose!".

"Yes, undoubtedly, and mighty awkward when you are well set with a pretty Miss to have a 15 incher drop outside your bedroom".

"Damn hard luck".

"Ay oh!" yawned Bill. "I'm turning in, going up at 3am".

"Same here" I replied and the droning of night planes soon sent us off to sleep.

27: Aerial combat and trench attacks

On the Gavrelle front the fighting had now relapsed into trench warfare once more, the Germans having brought up considerable numbers of men to check our recent activities.

Where only one or two lines of defence existed, preparations were pushed forward adding more lines of defence to form an effective barrier of trenches, barbed wire and strong points in the event of strong enemy retaliation. Working parties night and day worked upon these defences and it was not much of a "rest" to be out of the front line as one had the arduous job of trench digging, wiring, road making and a thousand other odd jobs to do besides.

"Believe me Ronnie, I'd sooner be in the trenches than these endless working parties" commented Jack Ferris to his nearest sweating pal.

"Begad so would I, you do get yer sleep, whereas while "resting" you get orders, orders, orders every bloomin' day and no damn - look out! Jerry coming".

Both chaps dumped themselves in the half-dug trench and waited until a plane zoomed low over their heads and spat out lead at the working party.

"The dirty cow" ejaculated Ronnie "that was a near thing".

"Yes, the swine, ought to tell us he's coming, I don't think!".

"Look Jack there he goes with one of our boys after him".

"And he'll catch him too".

"Jerry's climbing, got wind up!".

"Our chap is after him hot and strong".

"Now he's on top".

"Hello, Jerry is going to make a fight of it".

The two planes now circled, dived, climbed, spat lead and circled, climbed, dived, again and again, providing a good deal of excitement to the onlookers.

"Here come two more of our boys in Bristols" announced Sandy Martin nearby. "Good lads, now watch the fun".

"Our chap is done in" shouted Ronnie excitedly "he's coming down". And sure enough the British plane was falling rapidly to the ground out of control.

The German tried his best to make his escape, but the two new arrivals had by now flown between Jerry and his lines and a short sharp scrap brought him crashing to the ground not far from his first rival.

"Do you know Ronnie, I feel sorry for Jerry, couldn't expect to beat three of our chaps, and it seemed unsporting like to tackle him when he'd won his fight".

"Oh, that's war all over" replied Ronnie "can't be too fussy about numbers. If one man is beaten another two, or even a dozen, must do the job. Still I wouldn't care to take on three in one afternoon outing".

"I bet not Ronnie, but it would give you a good appetite for tea if you got through".

"Now, let's get digging old son, otherwise that Petty Officer is going to strafe us judging by the look in his eye".

June 12, dawned radiantly over the Gavrelle front, and although the Naval Division was spending a comparatively quiet morning, a terrific bombardment was going on away in the north where our boys were making a big attack. This attack meant, for the Royal Naval Division, a very arduous and monotonous spell of consolidating work on the Arras-Gavrelle front and some short fierce scrapping between Oppy and Gavrelle. The Germans, though very strong in defence, were nevertheless badly cared for in the way of equipment, arms and food which gave evidence of the severity of our gunfire in preventing their transport from reaching their trench lines.

Apart from purely local attacks and counter-attacks, the front line remained fairly stationary and this state of affairs carried on well into August. The attack up north, around Messines and Ypres, seemed to have been held up a bit and although in September the offensive was continued, the enemy were never "on the run". When the complete Russian collapse came about, fresh numbers of enemy troops and guns were transferred to the western theatre, as well as to the Italian front

96

where our allies had been making not inconsiderable progress against the partly exhausted and demoralised Austrians.

In order to keep things going in our favour fresh attacks had to be planned in Flanders and, for this reason, the Naval Division had to go North.

"We're in for Wipers[1] mates, and pull yer socks up, yer going to have some real scrapping now" commented a Petty Officer to his men one September morning.

"Anything for a change PO, they have different breeds of lice up there" was the answer from a wag.

"I say PO" chipped in Monty Blowers who must have been a pre-war nut "I suppose they have a jolly old canteen up there".

"One every 'undred yards, I don't think" answered the Petty Officer "and wot d' yer want with a canteen?".

"Only a fresh supply of pommade for my jolly old lice to eat and some brilliantine".

"You'll get all the pommade and brilliantine you want my lad, and you won't want a canteen either, Jerry will chuck it at yer every morning before breakfast".

"By Jove, aren't you cheerful PO, this beastly front has been bad enough, it won't be much worse".

"Wait and see my lad" was the cryptic rejoinder.

A month later Monty lay half buried in mud with sightless eyes staring to heaven; Bond Street, Piccadilly, Oxford Street and its environs will see him no more. Damned war.

---

1. Ypres

28: Ypres salient

The next few days the Division spent in preparing for a quick trek to Ypres. Everywhere men were becoming gloomy as the truth dawned on them, that still another winter was to be spent in France and the hopes of a quick finish during August and September were gone.

No longer were waggish remarks plastered on limbers and rail trucks such as during 1914-1916.

Notices such as "This way to Berlin", "Non-stop Berlin", "On the Spree to Berlin" etc. were never seen now as, during 1917, it became very apparent that no sudden crack up of enemy armies was to be expected and only constant, persistent and lengthy attacks of attrition were going to win through.

Tommy's sense of humour never left him, however, and instead of light-hearted, enthusiastic humour, a rather grim humour was brought to light in such remarks as "It's a ruddy limited company my lads"; "Too many people making money out of this, old cock"; "Must go on until all officers have VCs"; "Three years and duration"; "Pension when you're 60"; "Wonder who will be the last man alive" and so on. Then came the remark announced excitedly:

"The War - all over".

"All over?"

"Yes, all over France!".

The route taken to Ypres lay, in the first part, through pleasant French villages where the life experienced before the war seemed very little disturbed. Here was a large farmhouse situated amid a small wood of firs and beeches and the inevitable manure dump in the centre of the courtyard.

The farmer, a grey haired man with rosy face, stood at the gate looking with a sadness in his eyes at the troops passing on their way. Perhaps his thoughts were with the French and English boys who had passed this gate in the early days, when no one dreamed that so many tramping feet would have to pass along these straight French roads before the "job" was done.

Several "hands" were helping about the neighbouring fields, mostly women with just an old man or two, bent almost double by age and years of work on the land. A bright sun lit up this scene of rustic beauty, with a meandering stream alongside the road reflecting the tall poplars and deep blue sky. Further along the road evidences of war showed themselves in ripped tree trunks and broken walls, then we came to a village and rested for a meal.

So the troops wended their way like a snake through the fair countryside, doing its best to make men forget the horror of war for a few brief days. On the second day a division of the guards was passed.

"What's it like at Wipers mate?".

"Bloody awful" was the reply.

"Thanks, we're going to finish it, when we get there".

These and other bantering remarks were swung to and from the passing columns of men.

Nightfall and billets were found to rest weary limbs; Jack Ferris, with his platoon, in a large farmhouse barn and me, with the rest of the transport, in an outhouse of the same farm. The limbers and field kitchens were stacked in the yard and only the gleams of light from the windows of the farm lit up the scene. A solitary searchlight from some neighbouring hill swept across the sky like some ghostly arm reaching out after the unknown. The rest of the division was billeted in neighbouring farms and cottages in a nearby village.

Men moved about with the aid of candles, shielded from the night breeze by their hands, and, here and there, an electric torch showed up its white beam for an instant then disappeared. The barn was comfortable, well strawed and snug, and, after depositing my kit, I wandered into the night to take the horses to water at a nearby trough.

How glorious the night, how calm, with the sweet wind laden with country scents ruffling the hair and fanning the face. The only reminders of grim warfare were the dull thuds, borne on the wind, of distant guns.

After the drivers had watered and fed their horses, they turned into the farm barn for a "bit of eats" and a clean up with, last of all, a game of poker or banker.

29: Leave in Blighty

While everyone was busy a Chief Petty Officer strolled in and claimed full attention by announcing that "The following men are to fall in at 5pm sharp tomorrow evening in the roadway outside the farm. Equipment to be cleaned up and consist of belt or bandolier only. All buttons to be polished and boots blacked." Here followed the names and among them was mine. Those of us concerned were immediately full of questions: "What's up Chief?" "What's the job Chief?" "Are we to be shot at dawn?" "Is this for latrine duty Chief?" and similar questions.

The Chief Petty Officer looked around at the questioning faces and smiled, deliberately waiting for effect (he must have been an actor). Then snapped out the words "Leave draft". Needless to add the din that followed was deafening.

"Leave draft, ye gods".

"Just going to Wipers and then switched off to Blighty".

"Kiss me Chief!".

"Blighty! Boys - it's great".

They surrounded the Chief and plied him with hundreds of questions as to how, when, where and lots of other things besides. At last he made himself heard.

"All details will be given to you men tomorrow and, if any of you are drunk tonight, leave is cancelled".

"Right ho Chief, we'll be good".

"Good night lads".

"Good night Chief" and he was gone.

Jack Ferris hastened over to my side and patted me on the back. "Good luck Fred, hope you have a damned good time".

"Thanks Jack but I'm sorry you're not coming".

"Had my rest when I got wounded, shan't get my leave yet".

"Ye gods, it doesn't seem true yet Jack, to think of England and all it means after 17 months of active service".

"Ah, it's good your leave has come up before Ypres, eh Fred?"

"Yes Jack, nothing like making sure!".

The following evening came at last and one man was decidedly "bosky" so three of his pals polished up his equipment and clothes and dashed cold water in his face. He assembled with the others on the roadway, but it was a tremendous effort to keep upright despite the friendly shoulders either side of him.

The officer on duty inspected the men and stopped at the "bosky" one and looking hard into his eyes said "You're not drunk man, are you?".

"No shur" came the reply "I ain'tsh drunksh".

"Only the sun too hot today I suppose you damn fool" and as an aside to the men on either side of the "bosky" one "Keep him steady men, I'll let him go".

"Very well sir" replied the men "we'll take care of him". The officer handed the party over to a Petty Officer who was also bound for leave and they marched off.

"He's a sport, that officer" was a general comment "risking his job for that fool".

"I'll cure him when we get to the train" muttered one of his assistants.

When the station was eventually reached the cure was speedily effected for, with a fine left hook, the "bosky" one was felled to the platform, picked up roughly and knocked down again.

"'Arf a minitish, I ain't a punch ball" complained the aggrieved one.

"No, you're the biggest fool I've met" answered his assistant. "If you're not sober in two minutes I'll bash yer ruddy brains out".

He was soon sober and later cursed himself for the narrow shave he had of being left in billets.

The train (as is the way of leave trains) crawled through the darkening land, lit only at intervals by distant gun flashes which threw into relief the trees and houses of the quiet countryside. At times the train burst into a tornado of speed, doing quite 20 mph for five minutes, then relaxing into a still slower crawl as if ashamed of itself.

"Recommend me to a French troop train for taking away enthusiasm" I sighed to my Welsh pal sitting next to me.

"Let's sleep Lofty. It's the only thing to do".

One by one the occupants of the compartment dozed; it was only a sudden jolt and grinding of brakes that woke us with stiff joints and necks and feeling rather chilly, as is the custom after a sleep in a moving vehicle. A solitary oil lamp outside the carriage window denoted a platform and, on further inspection, it was found to be one of many platforms, in fact quite a fair-sized station. A French railway porter flung open doors and shouted "Abbeville" and what evidently meant "all change" as well.

"Well I'm damned, Abbeville of all places, thought we would be in Boulogne by now".

"Yus mate, and instead we ain't much nearer Boolong then when we first started".

An English officer came hurriedly onto the platform, formed up the English soldiers and informed them that they were to sleep in a large shed at the side of the railway until 5am when the train started for Boulogne.

"It's only 10pm now, so off to bed when you have had some supper; it will soon be time for your train" remarked the officer with a grin.

"What, stay the night here sir?" asked a voice.

"Yes I'm sorry but you've missed your connection".

At this news a lot of very uncomplimentary remarks about France and her railways were passed between the stranded leave draft men. When the shed was entered a further flow of fresh invective was hurled into space.

"Wot a bloody 'ole" was a comment from an enraged lad from West Ham. "No light, no beer and not even a bloody French tart to cheer us up. Ruddy Froggies!"

The officer soon reappeared with three men carrying hot coffee, rolls and cheese, purchased out of his own money. After these were disposed of the men felt a little more cheerful and, because they were informed that they were not allowed in the town, they made up several parties for cards played by the light of three porters lanterns which had been scrounged from the station's store.

As for me and Taffy Jenkins, we were quite content that we were on our way home and simply took this delay as still one more fresh experience among the many which swamped our young lives.

"Rather here than up the line 'eh Taffy?"

"Yes rather, and it's funny how some of those rough chaps make more fuss about a few hours in a dry railway hut than sitting in a sodden trench".

"It's a rum thing indeed Taffy, but most of us make more fuss about little things like a late train than we do if all hell is let loose around us."

"Yes Lofty, that's true; we British are a funny lot. Plunge us in Armageddon and we sing songs on our way to it, or tell smutty jokes while in it; but drop a fag in the mud and we swear and cuss like Satan himself. It's queer."

"What's your wire mattress like Taffy?"

"Pretty rotten, about three sound inches and the rest is all broken."

"Never mind, I'm so dog tired I can sleep on anything." And suiting actions to words I kicked my boots off, flung my tunic on a nail in the wall and putties under the wire bed and was soon wrapped in slumber plus an army blanket.

Taffy Jenkins soon followed suit and by midnight the hut was silent except for occasional sonorous snores and the squeak of rats that were outraged at this incursion on their usual haunts.

At 4.30am, we were awakened for coffee and biscuits and, after a wash under the engine pump, our leave party was all ready for the train for Boulogne. We arrived about 9am at Boulogne to find an air raid in progress and French anti-aircraft guns in action.

"Jerry is saying "au revoir" to us" commented Taffy Jenkins.

"I don't care as long as he leaves our boat alone; if he sinks that I shall curse" I replied.

"Here, have a cigarette Lofty and forget the war."

"Thanks."

Tired and dusty, we wound our way with the rest of the party to the harbour. Excitement ran high as the boat was boarded and we, at last, felt we were bound for Blighty. Always the fear of recall while on the train journey but, once on the boat and steaming out of the harbour on a calm October morning, everyone felt better and sure of their leave. Distant rumbles of guns troubled no one and in each face was a happy reflection of their thoughts. Men did not speak much, each was too busy picturing mothers, wives, sweethearts awaiting them in that land, at present just a misty line on the horizon. How good to be going home when only a few hours ago it seemed they would never see England again. No little cause for wonder that when men landed at Folkestone harbour they gazed in an almost bewildered way at its familiar leas, pier and promenade, hardly able to realise that for 10 whole days the "horror" was left behind them and they were to meet their loved ones. Turn away your gaze, for that hefty miner lad from Northumberland and that Cockney boy have moist tears in their eyes.

As we stepped off the ship the raucous voice of a Sergeant Major greeted us with instructions about our train (even Sergeant Majors have their uses sometimes). At once the flow of our thoughts was snapped and with a joyous yelp we boarded the train. This train, unlike the French trains, got a move on and we were in London in less than $2^1/_2$ hours.

At Charing Cross everyone hurried away in different directions and the leave began in earnest. Nine full days of reunion, celebration, joyous greetings and fun, except where a sad note is sounded by the news of a brother's death at the "front" or where a woman, with a sweet sad face, has so little money to spare that even her boy's homecoming cannot be celebrated as royally as she would wish. Even in these circumstances a great well of joy and happiness is filled to overflowing and a quiet restful time in each other's company satisfies them both.

No war is mentioned during the first day or two, only a close embrace and "How are you my boy?" answered by "Fine thanks" is the first greeting.

Nine days of forgetfulness.

Air raids, food rationed, political strife and strikes; who cares?

Nine days of bliss.

A mother's arm round one's waist, a father's handshake, a sweetheart's warm moist kisses.

Nine days of heaven.

The sweet strains of an organ, mellow as the sunset, the quiet singing of a choir, the sympathetic voice of the preacher, brought balm to my heart and mind on my first Sunday evening in England. The full church of worshippers, and during the collection the playing of Beethoven's "Adagio Cantabile from Pianoforte Sonata" quite effected the work of restoration and made me feel that still God was remembered and revered, despite all the clash of arms and confusion "over there".

My parents and, last but not least, my sweetheart all saw to it that my leave should be a never-to-be-forgotten time and, although it would make the parting harder, it would leave many happy and tender memories to treasure during times of hardship. It was on this leave that Florence Allen became "my girl". The evenings when we wandered alone through well-remembered and familiar country lanes and fields, and a bright moon turning night into day, are not to be described because to us young folk it was heaven and therefore too sacred to bring to the publicity of general conversation. Florence had her hero, and I my heroine, and we leave it at that.

Every good, as well as every bad, thing ends and the partings were sharp-edged with sorrow. Florence said goodbye to me that night, not trusting herself to be at the station next morning. My parents saw me off and mother (as nearly all mothers did) kept a smiling face to the end only, somehow, the lips would twitch so, and the eyes would mist over. Father kept his end up too, but the handclasp was long and lingering. I dared not trust myself to say much.

Hundreds of stony-faced soldiers were on my train, everyone seemed under great strain, and what made things harder was the presence of one poor wife who cried and clung to her husband's neck unable to control the immense grief at parting. Some kind friend took her in their arms and led her away as the train started. Handkerchiefs were waved, hats were raised and men stood bareheaded as the train rolled out from the station. Those same handkerchiefs a moment later were in use for purposes other than waving. Those fathers were staring dry-eyed and hopeless at the end of the train; and in the train, men could not speak until long after London had faded from view.

30: Passchendaele

Jack Ferris was sitting in the shell-hole on Passchendaele Ridge eating a few 'dog' biscuits and a bit of dried bully beef. It was night and all around lay muddied figures in shell-holes. Not even a decent trench could be dug, as it would fill quickly with the slimy mud, which abounded everywhere and literally caked everything, from the brass buttons on a man's tunic to his very soul.

Out of the pitchy black, lit only by occasional starshells which spluttered in the rain, came hurtling the shells that went plop! plop! into the soddened morass and churned yet another hole, soon to be partially obliterated by a near neighbour of more recent origin.

"It's hopeless this infernal mud" whispered Jack Ferris to the other occupants of the shell-hole "one thinks mud, eats mud, reeks of mud and sleeps in mud - then they tell us to advance!"

"You volunteered for it mate" came a voice out of the dark.

"Right old man, I volunteered to fight, but I didn't volunteer to eat France or even bathe in it!"

Conditions were indeed appalling. The road from Poperinghe to Ypres was bad, but the other roads leading from Ypres to the "line" were now but ploughed tracks, well sprinkled with shell holes, dead horses and men. Only after leaving these tracks could men advance. Not even a packhorse could find a footing so all sandbags, ammunition, food and a thousand and one necessities of war had to be man-handled over a considerable area. Later in October trench boards had to be laid down and even they were, in places, sucked into the morass.

Woe betide the man with a heavy burden who lost his foothold on the trench boards - he became immersed up to the waist and, in some cases lost his life, for sheer fatigue prevented him from making good his escape from the bog into which he was slowly sucked. Add to this a heavy artillery bombardment on a pitch-black night with rain still steadily falling and you have a picture of Passchendaele and the surroundings.

After the early Autumn advances, any possibility of fighting the enemy seemed out of the question. As one man tersely put it "You can't advance, you can't retire, you can only darn well stay where you are and sink".

Even the dead men and horses lying about Passchendaele ridge and its surrounding valleys could not be buried. They were gradually sucked into the mire and so out of sight - buried by nature's own hand.

Despite these almost unbearable conditions, the Royal Naval Division bravely upheld the traditions of the senior service and gave an excellent account of themselves when advancing by slow, laborious stages over the swamps and low lying lands around Passchendaele Ridge. The Marines and Canadians on either side also did some daring work and made quite considerable progress against a stubborn enemy who shifted his strong points overnight so that our artillery could never quite succeed in paving a smooth way for the infantry.

Advances in these conditions were a matter of yards only, but during October about 1,000 yards of territory was captured on a rough frontage of 2,000 yards. This territory included Bray, Varlet and Sourd Farms, now but heaps of rubbish; Banff House and a part of the Paddebeek, a smaller stream of unimportant size but a stumbling block to our advance as the Germans had it well marked by machine guns and artillery.

It is useless to pick out any battalion for special praise as each one suffered severely and did valiant deeds. On one of the advances in early morning, a whole company of Artists Rifles was entirely annihilated. Into this inferno I returned from leave and after much seeking and enquiries found the horse lines and camp of the Howe Battalion, pitched on the edge of a small wood just a little to the north of Ypres.

Weird and haggard against the greying evening sky stood the gaunt spectre of the Cloth Hall at Ypres and battered ruins surrounded it as if clinging near it for sheer comforts sake.

Limbers and gun carriages rattled along the roads and rats scurried among the ruins. Proud Ypres was a deserted town at night, save for the life given to it by shells crashing into it and breaking into still smaller pieces the debris of what was once a prosperous town of happy people.

The next saddest sight on earth after a deserted battlefield must surely be a smashed town, especially at eventime, when any man with the least imagination could conjure up visions of what once was, and compare it with its present state.

As two officers, walking together down its main road, observed the dreariness and waste of it all, one remarked that it put a lump in his throat and the other could not reply for very sadness. A moment or two later, one was lying dead and mangled and the other gasping his last breaths, for a sudden shell had caught them unprepared. Ypres, dear city of memories and tranquillity, now lying in ruin, the grave of thousands of our boys.

To me it was somewhat of a nightmare this first evening back in Flanders; not a little homesick, my best pal Jack Ferris up at the front line (or what was left of it), the transport all absent from camp taking rations up to the reserve trenches, and only cook to talk to. Cook's conversation was not very intelligent as he was busy preparing the evening meal, but the scent of cooking food and a dixie of hot tea brought a look of pleasure to my face as I was desperately hungry and thirsty, and very weary after my 12 mile tramp from railhead.

A dog came towards me with a huge rat in his mouth, and after dropping it at my feet, barked joyously at cook and was rewarded by a saucer of milk and a bone. "Poor devil" ruminated cook "he's a stray dog that's been wandering around this camp for days. I heard the other day that he lived with his master in Ypres until the family was wiped out by shellfire and now he wanders disconsolately round the town trying to earn a doggie living by killing rats and getting tasty scraps of food for a reward. Poor devil".

"Tragic I call it" I said lighting up a cigarette as I spoke. "Poor little beggar, you didn't deserve this fate did you old boy?" patting his head as I spoke. And the dog cocked his head sideways and then drooped his head as if he understood in his doggie mind that he had someone's sympathy.

"When are our boys coming down Cookie?".

"Tomorrow I expect, A Company has had a rough time so I don't think its much good ordering more than 80 rations".

"Ye Gods! as bad as that?".

"Yus, Corny, and lucky if there are 80 men left in the Company".

"Good God!"

A rattle of wheels and horses hooves on the road outside announced the return of the transport limbers. I went outside to exchange greetings with my old comrades and helped to unhitch the horses and feed and water them. This done, the drivers entered the mess tent with their dixies and for the next five minutes "Cookie" was kept very busy.

"How's the front line tonight George?" I asked of a lean figure, mud-splashed and weary, yet enjoying his repast to the full. A moment elapsed whilst George wrestled with a tin opener and a can of fruit.

"Quiet old son, too quiet for me, hope the boys won't cop out tomorrow when they are relieved".

"I never like quiet nights" I remarked. "Generally the forerunners of a strafe".

"Yus, Corny old son, this is a rotten hole, too exciting for my liking, and the horses, poor devils, are getting overworked. Only about one mile of good road, then clay and muck sucks them down and makes the poor beasts sweat heavily. Damn shame I call it, to take them up night after night without a rest".

"You always were tender hearted towards your horses" chipped in another occupant of the tent, "it doesn't pay to think about them too much".

"Can't help it" countered George "they didn't ask for this bloody trouble and they don't deserve to be worked to death. Why, tonight old Nigger was so exhausted he laid down immediately I tied him up and it takes some work, believe me, to make a horse lay down before he's had his grub. Poor blighter was done in almost".

"Never mind George" put in Cookie "I'll give him some porridge before I turn in".

"Don't you have any sympathy for Nigger? Your porridge would put him right out!"

"Rot, you can't beat it George".

"Can't eat it, yer mean!"

There followed remarks from all the others as to the merits of Cookie's cooking. Only when Cookie produced a bottle of whisky did he escape the criticism of the drivers. That whisky soon disappeared.

31: Poperinghe and more killing

On the morrow the transport were all out early to bring down the battalion from the line and only I was left in the camp with the cooks to provide for the boys when they returned.

Later I was sent to Poperinghe to get some more supplies. Mounting my old pal Daisy, I was soon in a hard canter down the cobbled road into the quaint town of Poperinghe. Here I found the town much as usual, with French civilians going about their daily duties in fields and gardens, and only a few damaged houses told of long-distance shells finding a billet. A great number of the better class houses had green shutters closed across the windows and the gardens looked deserted, their owners having evidently departed when the Germans approached so near to their neighbourhood as Ypres. A large building was now the home of a YMCA depot; and the square, cobble-stoned and with Council Chamber and Church on different sides, was the temporary home of army wagons and limbers of all types. Estaminets were open and old men and women, who with their families had refused to desert their homes when invasion had threatened, were to be seen about the streets and cottage gardens quite oblivious (or apparently so) to the fact that the greatest battlefield ever known was only a few miles away and a sudden breakthrough by the enemy would imperil their lives and homes.

I entered the army stores and obtained satisfaction of my requirements by means of the presentation of a chit. Everything in the war was obtained by a chit, signed usually by an officer, requesting anything from a needle and thread to a howitzer, or from a horse to a tin of bully beef.

Returning by way of Ypres main road I was surprised to find a small chalet open quite near Ypres and a charming French girl and her mother serving the inevitable eggs on chips, chocolate and coffee to any soldier, driver or any other rank who happened to be passing.

I dismounted, and tying Daisy to the gate, went into the small garden and sat at one of the tables, enjoyed a plate of eggs and ham with good French coffee and engaged in lively conversation with the French proprietress.

"Are you not nervous Mademoiselle so near the line as this?" I asked.

"No, no, Monsieur, it ees quite safe here and only a few leetle shells come plop into the fields near" answered Jeanette with a laugh.

"Leetle shells" sighed her mother "they make my house, what you call it, tremible, but Jeanette she not afraid, she say what is good enough for Papa, good enough for her. He is a soldier and quite near Verdun now".

"Is your father still alive Jeanette?"

"Oui Monsieur, still alive, but we dread what each day will bring by post".

"Wish him the best of luck from me".

"Tank you Meester Soldier, and I hope you nevaire will get hurt" answered Jeanette.

"You deserve a good trade for your pluck".

"Oh the Tommies come here lots and they are very nice and spend quite all their money, don't they Maman?".

"Oui Jeanette, and always the same thing they say. 'How's the brave leetle Ma'm'selle today?'".

At this praise from her mother Jeanette smiled and blushed and talked rapidly in French with those pretty gestures of the hands and shoulders so becoming to the French girl and woman. Evidently scolding her mother, I thought. Her mother laughed and hurried away with mock fear on her face to attend other newcomers. Just a little sketch of the Frenchwomen's pluck and daring, and absolute disregard for safety so long as they kept the little home intact and saved a few francs for the hoped-for homecoming of their lover, husband or father.

I left reluctantly to return to camp and learned on my arrival that the 'boys' were on their way down, having been relieved early in the morning. It was now about 11am and soon a small group of men were observed coming down the road. I went toward them to check whether they were the advance guard of my battalion and recognised my pal Jack Ferris among them. This little party, mud-caked, dirty, bedraggled with unshaven faces, and almost a look of insanity in their eyes, was not the advance guard, but A Company in its entirety.

"Jack old chap it's me" I said.

A wild-eyed stare, then in a dull voice "Hello Corny, you back? Had a good time?" asked Jack.

"Yes, old man, thanks. You've had a rough house".

"Don't mention it".

"Where's the Company Jack?".

"We are the Company".

"Good God".

"Yes, 18 left, and half insane at that".

"Poor devils; everyone else gone?".

"Everyone".

"Killed?"

"Mostly, and those wounded prayed for it and were glad they got it. We properly got it in the neck".

Seeing the distress in my friend's eyes I changed into light conversation.

"Jack old chap, come to my tent, I've got some good grub and hot coffee and rum".

"Fine Fred, you're a sport".

In the tent we talked of everything except war and, after a good meal (treble rations were available owing to the small number of survivors), cigarettes were produced and the comforting fumes brought consolation to both of us. Rum and coffee in abundance brought life and sanity back to Jack Ferris and he opened up in confidence to me.

"Do you know Corny, this war is bloody, there's no other description. Mud, mud, mud, bullets, shells and rain, gets right into one's soul and ruins it. Jerry's as bad as us, and the poor devils we captured two nights ago, seems like two years ago, were pitiful to look at. Half starved, wet, shell-shocked, some crying and yet they didn't ask for war any more than we did. I gave them some of my wet fags and they looked scared. Thought we should let them smoke, I suppose, and then shoot them".

"Poor sods".

"Yes, I agree, and yet they are our enemy and we must go on killing them, or be killed, 'til some bleedin' War Lord or Prime Minister says "Stop". Christian countries at war, and yet the savages in Africa and elsewhere would look like gentlemen compared to us. It's ironical to think of English, French and German missionaries going out to convert them. Convert them to our way of life" blazed Jack. "It's damnably funny and yet tragic".

"Wish God would step in and stop this foolishness Jack".

"Why should he Fred, the nations of Europe started it, mankind must be taught a lesson, so it seems to me, and as all of us are so darned conceited and proud, I mean nationally of course, it seems we have got to learn the lesson of Christianity and brotherliness through blood and suffering. And I bet you Fred, that after this war is over, if anyone is left alive, they will again start building large guns, aeroplanes, battleships and tanks just to prove, once and for all, what fools men are. War to end war! That's just bosh and blather, like saying bath to end bathing! One wash and we are clean for ever is nonsense and, unless men of all nations learn to be pals, there will be another war larger than this. Think of all the hatred this war is going to leave in its wake. Suppose Germany wins, are we going to call them brothers and live happily with them? Not likely! And the same thing applies if we win. Although Christ lived nearly 2,000 years ago, He is still mentally and spiritually 10,000 years ahead of mankind, and this war proves it".

"But Jack don't you think the common men of each nation would be pals if their leaders let them?".

"Yes, perhaps, but their nationality is still too strong a thing to enable them to think internationally".

"Perhaps you're right".

"Let's go for a walk Fred, I want a bath badly".

"I know the place Jack, get a towel and we'll go now".

32: The routine of war

For the next four days the remnants of the Howe battalion enjoyed the brief respite in visits to Poperinghe and neighbouring YMCA and church army huts, where the usual games were available together with refreshments.

During these four days the look of horror and insanity left the faces of the men and they resumed a more composed appearance. Kits were replenished, uniforms cleaned and fresh reinforcements were sent to help make up the battalion to war strength. Only a distant bombardment or occasional air-raid disturbed the rest, and duties were of the lightest.

On the fourth night, orders were issued for a return to the front and the usual scene of activity was witnessed. Water bottles filled, mostly with water, but occasionally with something stronger, equipment polished up, rifles cleaned, ammunition issued and curses and ribald jokes indulged, the latter to hide the fear in each heart.

Ten thirty pm and only snores rent the air, for at 3.00am reveille and the unknown, so men slept and only the noises from the cook's galley announced that worthy as being prepared for an early breakfast.

Three o'clock on a foggy morning and the shrill notes of a bugle; five minutes later flickering candles are lit, one after another inside the tents, throwing the shadows of the occupants on the canvas and reminding one of the shadowgraphs children delight in. A few minutes elapse and shirted figures run to the washing trough and splash and gasp for a few moments before briskly towelling. Shaving had been attended to overnight, for who can shave in ice-cold water at 3.00am with numb fingers and dull razor blades.

The appetising smell of sizzling bacon emanated from the cook's galley and soon eager hands are holding out dixie lids for a rasher and some bread and the dixie itself for some tea, hot and sweet and life-invigorating.

At 3.45am dark figures are lined up on the road, officers appear from the dense darkness around, quiet orders are given and obeyed, and like ghosts the men move off to the trenches. "Taking over" at 5.00am, or come to that at any time, is a clever business, for even when well-defined trenches are available, some post or dugout is nearly always overlooked. In the case of Passchendaele, where there were only mud-filled holes and craters available, it is a wonder that men ever came to be found and relieved. To find a named street, by daylight, in a well-ordered town is not always easy; to find an unnamed shell-hole, by night, with a thick fog around, is sheer wizardry.

The transport followed with supplies and, to me, the way was unknown so I let my horses have their head and, scenting rather than seeing the way, they arrived at the dump. From there the unloading party had to carry these supplies, across seemingly unending miles of duckboards, to the troops in the reserves and outposts. The night had, up until now, been quiet and any sounds were muffled by the fog but, suddenly, the darkness was stabbed by bright flashes and dull thuds and I found it weird in the extreme to hear the progress of an artillery duel; to know that out of the fog, at any moment, might come a splinter of shell to stop my life or kill my horses.

The ghostly figures of men moving about unloading limbers, the rattle of wheels of passing transport only dimly seen, though but 10 feet away, the unending wails and shrieks of shells passing overhead, stretcher bearers passing by with their loads of mangled humanity, stamped itself into the mind for ever.

A tall figure approached to the horses' heads and signalled me to get moving again so, with alacrity, I turned my horses in the direction of camp. Both I and my horses were sweating profusely though the night was cold and the drive back was a nightmare. No feeling of comradeship, as at the dump where men were talking and unloading, but a lonely ride in fog and shell bursts all around, and only the comfort of a fag-end now glowing brightly one inch from the tip of my nose.

Eight different stops to enquire of some passing phantom the way back, and eventually camp was reached. The horses were safely hitched to the line and fed and I sought the comfort of my blanket for four brief hours, after having tasted some excellent coffee Cookie had prepared for the night duty men.

On active service no time is lost trying to woo sleep, it comes immediately and the exhausted one no sooner lies down, than thought is dead.

Day-after-day the usual routine of harness cleaning, grooming, feeding, and fetching supplies from the rear. Night-after-night taking the supplies to the front line, or as near as possible. In this sector it meant some mile or more away owing to lack of good roads.

On one sunny afternoon in early November, Peters, Henderson and myself were detailed for transport work on a road well advanced to the front line and, proceeding with our horsed limbers along this road, wooded country on either side, we were at peace with the world. No guns firing, a mellow sunshine, cigarettes to smoke, a "cushy" job, provided Peters with the remark "Like Rotten Row on Sunday".

An ambulance went tearing past and, when about 100 yards ahead, became enveloped in a cloud of smoke - a deafening crash and, when the atmosphere cleared, a little wreckage lying about was all that was left of an army ambulance.

"My God!! Poor devils" muttered Peters, white to the lips. We searched for any possible live body but found none.

"A direct hit" commented Henderson "and no warning".

"Let's go" I suggested "I feel sick".

Silently mounting we proceeded and reported the matter later.

War in its most cold-blooded aspect, a sunny afternoon, all quiet, a sudden shell, a few rent bodies, a crushed vehicle. All quiet again.

A camp of wooden huts, surrounded with two feet high mud banks for protection, some men engaged in a clean up, some in games, some in sleep. Everything quiet; a low drone, three deafening crashes, eighteen riddled bodies, and the angel in the sky has had a good afternoon's sport, and the name of the game is "bombing enemy camp". All quiet again except for groans and cries from stricken humans who crawl in agony and collapse and die.

33: Welsh Ridge and Fins

Before mid-November the Royal Naval Division was withdrawn from the Passchendaele battlefield and was ordered to the Cambrai sector, where the enemy was making a very successful attack upon our front line positions.

Welsh Ridge was the next battleground and, although a very sharp salient, the Division was to strengthen it and hold, as the Ridge commanded a very fine view of the enemy strongholds and important centres. On a sharp frosty night with a slight mist the Howe battalion went into the line and the transport, stationed in a small townlet of Fins, prepared to follow with provisions. Two wooden army huts and three old French stables formed the transport headquarters. Following a rather bad road to Metz-en-Couture, a fairly important country town at one time but now very battered by shellfire, the horses had a steep pull up a long hill to the crest which gave, by day, a very extensive view of the country. At the top of the crest the road divided, one straight on to Ribecourt-la-Tour and a branch to the right to Beaucamp, now a mass of broken walls and timber. Seen on a misty night it presented a weird and very saddening sight.

However, one became used to shattered villages and towns, and only a short, passing depression would trouble the mind. The open country, ploughed by shell bursts and bereft of bushes, trees or fences, was preferable to the ruins. The limbers followed in single file, in unending line, up and down the narrow country road. The bobbing heads of steel-hatted drivers, the steady footfalls of horses' hooves and the hard rattle of limber wheels on a frost-bound road were passing impressions of this night ride. The road sank below field level and on the banked sides were deep dugouts, which had been made by the Germans, and credit must be given to them for the solidity and comfort of their dugouts, and the depth and roominess of most.

"Them bleedin' Jerries must 'ave thought they were 'ere for good" muttered one of the drivers, eyeing the entrances with longing.

"This blasted war is here for good mate" came a reply in front.

"So is the louses" chortled from the rear. A general laugh, and on the limbers clattered until they came to what appeared to be, by night's uncertain vision, a large dumping ground, with a small ridge running alongside with cuttings in its side, denoting trenches. Here the limbers were unloaded to the relief of the drivers who were noting without pleasure that shells of small calibre were coming over much more frequently, heralds of a coming storm.

Scarcely had the last limber unloaded when the artillery storm broke in all its usual fury, challenge answered by challenge. The valley became wreathed in smoke and Welsh Ridge seemed on fire. The shouted orders of transport officers, the quick retirement of lorries and limbers, the shouts for stretcher bearers, the screams of hit horses, the moans of de-limbed men, the constant din of bursting shells and the rattle of machine guns a few hundred yards away, made hell itself seem a desirable place.

I kept my horses well in check and, although sweating with fear, I gave no outward sign except to keep low in the saddle. The sunken road afforded some shelter, but out on the Ridge again it was very unhealthy, and not until Metz was reached could the transport feel themselves safe. Back areas were being shelled as well as the trench lines and so it was with feelings of thankfulness and relief that the quiet of Fins was reached at 2:00am, with flakes of snow beginning to fall. Ears still deafened by the bombardment failed to hear a bombing raid in progress nearby. It was not until an anti-aircraft gun close to the stables started banging away at the German plane that showed up in a searchlight beam like a white moth, that the drivers once more took their horses out on to the road to avoid a possible stampede in the stables.

The raid over, horses were fed and stabled and the exhausted men, too tired to talk, flung themselves down in the wooden huts to get what little sleep they could before dawn. Luckily no casualties were reported in the Howe transport but some severe cases were heard of in regard to the other transports caught in that little valley near Welsh Ridge.

The white world which greeted my eyes when I woke next morning set me afire with the desire for mischief and, going outside the hut, I

119

collected some snowballs and distributed them among the other inhabitants of the hut. In three minutes a snowball fight was in full swing outside the hut, amid laughter and splutterings. Only the call to duty of watering the horses stopped the fun. Little amusements and carefree moments like these kept men sane and everywhere in the battle zones men took the fun as and when it came. No good waiting for your joy, alive at 7:00am, one might be a corpse at 7.05am by a little bolt of danger from out of the sky.

After attending the horses, a mad dash to cook's galley took place and sizzling bacon, bread and hot tea found ready customers. No bacon every tasted so delicious in civil life, but then, of course, danger did not add the spice to it, and on a snowy morning a man had nothing to do before breakfast but wash and shave. It is surprising how the unimportant things of that past life became so important in this new life and important matters became of no importance. A hand of cards, a song, a drink, a letter from home, a parcel of good things, a clean shirt, a sharp razor were all very important "out there"; at home they were of no importance.

A clean collar, perfect necktie, maidens' glances, the 8.35am train to town, the boss, and the annual rise in salary. How insignificant "out there"! Talking of increases in salary, a story was told of how a Munster Fusilier captured three Germans single-handed and insisted on presenting them to his Colonel personally, with a request for an increase in wages! Habit is strong.

One bright sunny day, snow carpeted the ground and in the frosty air two planes indulged in a fight over Fins. Soon one came down in flames, the pilot flinging himself out and crashing head first in an adjacent field, his flaming plane fluttering earthwards like a stricken bird. When some of the transport men reached this pilot he was buried up to his waist in the ground and only his shattered trunk and legs remained visible. It was a slightly built German youth and our boys were too sympathetic to rejoice at our airman's victory. They quietly buried the German pilot and placed a small piece of wood at his head to mark the spot. His few papers and books they took to the transport office for identification. An unfinished letter to his sweetheart was among his papers so, in a few days' time, some sweet German girl would be mourning for her lover. Our newspapers printed such rubbish about the 'Huns' and the women that gave birth to them, that it came as a shock to realise that they were men and women like ourselves, knowing sorrow and joy in the same way and feeling as horrified at the ravages of war as we did. Certain of the race, in the heat and latitude of war, became beasts but 5% does not make a nation, else we should not be over-virtuous ourselves.

That same night four men were detailed for various duties with the limbers up the line. Garnett and I were sent with one lorry, on a gruesome errand to the reserve trenches, to bring away the headless body of a certain Commander who was killed in a shell burst at the dugout exit. When the main road was reached, which was among the ruins of Trescault, we each lit a cigarette to steady our shaky nerves. It was with a great feeling of companionship that I watched all the bobbing, glowing red cigarette ends of various drivers as they passed up and down the road to Hell. Funny little red glowing ends, but they were a solace to nerves all taut and afraid.

The weary old year closed and 1918 dawned without hope. The world was weary and hopeless, it seemed eternity since men had lived decently and with peace in their hearts.

In their billets at Fins, men of the Howe transport talked of the New Year without enthusiasm.

"Well lads it's a graun New Year".

"Glad you like it Scotty".

"What's up the noo, are ye no satisfied?".

"Satisfied with it? To 'ell! What's good about it? - mud, snow, jam, bread, tea, snow, mud, rain, bread, jam, tea - all the same bleedin' menu we've had for three bloody years".

"Och, awa wid ye mon, ye are nigh crazy, it's a guid life, plenty girls, smokes, guid food, clouts to wear, aal for nathin - some of ye are niver satisfied".

"Cheer up me hearties" broke in a voice from under a horse's belly "war's going to end this year".

"Who told you?"

"My big sister".

"Well bring your big sister on here, I'll show her where the war will end".

"You couldn't show a girl anything this frosty weather".

"Oh couldn't I? Anyway I bet you any money you like".

"Shut up you rude sods" broke in the voice of the Petty Officer "always talking about things you can't eat" - laughter from the ranks!

"I say PO, did you hear the tale of the curate who visited a pretty bird ....?"

"Shut up Ginger, my 'orse is listening to yer".

"Alright men, pack up" answered the PO "have a sing-song in the hut and I'll bring along some beer for you".

"Hoorah, we'll be there PO, trust us".

"Will ye no agree it's a guid year the noo?".

"Yus, Scotty old son, it is".

And the party left the stables and crossed over the road to the wooden hut which, if devoid of furniture, had a good fire and a stove and kept out the intense cold.

34: A friend is killed

The early months of the new year were spent by the whole Division in various raids on the German lines and the repulsing of strong counter-attacks. The enemy artillery seemed to be particularly strong of late, and very successfully dealt with our strong points and support lines, obliterating trenches and smashing our wire entanglements.

When the various battalions were out of the line for a brief spell, they were engaged in digging fresh trenches as defence lines some few miles behind the front lines. Havringcourt Wood, the grave of many gallant hearts, Ruyaulcourt, Metz, Ytres, Equancourt, Etricourt, Bus and Bertincourt all housed companies of men who were engaged in these new defence lines. Jack Ferris met me on one of these working parties and, not having met for some weeks, we had a considerable amount of news to discuss within a short time.

"Hey Corny, still alive?".

"Yes Jack, how do?" I asked clasping his hands.

"It's good to see you old son".

"Same here."

"Don't like the look of things Fred, all this trench digging business, looks to me as if we expect trouble".

"I think you're right Jacko, our transport has been taking up an awful lot of ammunition lately, and I heard a rumour this morning that they are breaking up the Howe battalion and dividing us amongst the other battalions".

"Don't like the sound of it at all".

"Ah well Jack, we've been through it before so we should be getting hardened to anything that comes along now".

"How is Flo old man?" asked Jack.

"Fairly fit when last I heard, except for those cursed Zepp raids which upset the nerves of the old folk. Darn rotten to think they must be made to suffer so badly and dread to see a fine starlight night".

"Yes Fred, it's a wonderful thing, a heroic deed to bomb helpless girls, old folk and children who haven't even a pea shooter for defence. It shows how civilised we are old son".

"Don't get too harsh and cynical Jack, we must try to keep some little faith in the ultimate good in mankind, though its very hard at times to realise this fact. How is Ruth, and when are you going to marry her?".

"God alone knows old man, I had my leave cancelled last week, so must be content with letters. She keeps well, Fred, and so far as I know is still at Etaples. Wish I could see her for a weekend; I badly need some of her kisses to cheer me up".

"Rotten luck about your leave Jack, I am sorry. Try to keep cheerful old boy. We're still alive and kicking. Anyway I must go now but pop over to my billet tonight and have some juice. You'll find our transport limber in the third barnyard on the left at Ruyaulcourt, and at the back of the yard are two barns, ours is the right one. Not such good billets as at Fins, but it's near a canteen".

"Thanks Fred, I'll come."

"Cheerio".

"Cheerio".

Five minutes later Jack Ferris lay dead and several more of the working party seriously wounded. A German Fokker, a swoop to earth, short burst of machine gun fire and many good lads lying around.

That night two of us were disconsolate, I'd lost my second closest pal and Ruth her lover. She received the army telegram whilst on duty and within two minutes a white-faced girl had to smile to cheer a wounded patient while her heart was breaking. Only when she came off duty did she break down utterly and completely in the privacy of her quarters while a sympathetic pal made her a cup of tea.

I wrote her a letter later on suggesting that we meet in a few months' time to give each other comfort over a mutual tragedy in our lives.

I had no heart left for my duties and only did my work in a mechanical, dazed way for some days, not caring if the end came or not. Warned by officers twice for riding to the danger of my horses in shellfire, I suddenly seemed to awake and old Sooty, my horse, had the strange experience that evening of having me hanging around his neck sobbing bitterly without tears.

My case was one of many where pals had become so strong in friendship that the loss of one means heartbreak and in not a few cases a definite mental injury. Only the urgency of war and the fresh air life brought me back to normal.

Men were pals indeed in France, and no civil life friendship ever became so deep. More surface friendship, less real root, hence a nicely worded phrase and a subscription for a wreath, no more. In France no wreath, no phrase, only dumb grief.

35: The German Spring Offensive

February turned to go, March entered and a brooding silence reigned over the whole of the Cambrai front. The gathering storm gave no indication to the average Tommy that soon the whole of the line from the Atlantic Ocean to the Swiss frontier would be aflame with the enemy's guns, nor that English and French armies would be rolled up, like one rolls a cigarette paper. To some, especially the officers, this brooding, sullen silence was full of foreboding and misgiving. To the men it was a relief from the severe local attacks and counter-attacks that had continued almost daily throughout the last three months.

The corps headquarters staff were feverishly calling for fresh reserves, more guns, more ammunition, more working parties to dig reserve lines for defence, and knowing all the while that the enemy was massing in great numbers all along the western front. There seemed no end to the reserves in men and guns which Germany was flinging into the line, judging by aeroplane observation and the reports of prisoners who were taken in surprise raids.

Three to one, four to one, five to one .... So mounted the odds against us in early March and we were powerless to prevent the coming crash.

To make a few more available men, one battalion in every four was transferred to the other three battalions, thus saving the transport men for the fighting line and also releasing odd staff men, miners, cyclists and canteen helpers for the front line. In fact many of these men who had participated in these other innumerable duties in the back areas, now found themselves with a rifle in their hands and felt mighty strange with it. All the old rules about rifle cleaning, firing and bayonet work had to be hastily produced from the dim memories of two or three years ago.

I was drafted to the Drake battalion and once again took rifle and pack in place of reins and fodder. I missed my horse pals rather keenly and felt strangely out of place in a new battalion with new faces all around me. The officers were not familiar, as when I was last in the Drake battalion I had only just landed in France, and practically the whole personnel of the battalion had changed through two years of active service. I did see one or two men of the "Howe", but for the most part my old battalion was scattered broadcast and all old associations broken.

The billets were tents and huts on the edge of Havrincourt Wood and in the wood itself were innumerable dugouts, disused entrenchments and strong points. A short wander among the blasted bushes and trees, now beginning to show innumerable points of green, revealed to the keen observers evidences of past sanguinary encounters: steel hats of German and English pattern were half buried in dead leaves and showed dents and holes where shrapnel had pierced; hand grenades, now rusted, which had dropped from some hand suddenly become lifeless; old rifles; bits of shell and entrenching tools left lying beside a heap of earth, where some heroic soul had endeavoured to scratch a small protection in the earth, before meeting his end, without completing his task. Sundry odd gas masks with torn tubes and broken bands, denoting fierce hand-to-hand conflict, seemed out of place in this now peaceful spot given over to many small camp fires with earnest young faces intent on the warming contents of dixies. As dusk drew on, activity died down and men retired to tents and huts to sing a song, play a hand of cards, polish equipment or read according to inclination or dictates of duty.

A bright night sky completed a picture, full of mystery and romance and brooding. Only an occasional Verey light or distant flash of guns told of the horror of a few miles away where men crouched in holes, sweating and fearful, or gazed into nothingness looking for an unseen enemy.

The weary monotony of trench digging parties ended and we marched with the battalion across the countryside towards the front line and Ribecourt. It was evening and the sun was setting in a hazy red light, leaving the countryside bathed in mellow radiance with a sad dusk following. Gradually the gun flashes became more pronounced as night came on, star shells ascended and Verey lights spluttered in the vault of heaven. Dusky figures in steel helmets, with equipment tightened up to prevent noise, moved in small parties across the fields past Trescault, like ghosts bent on some eerie errand. Soon a steep rise in the ground and the crest of a ridge was reached; along this crest ran the old Hindenburg line, strong in dugouts and vantage points. Here the road to Ribecourt was taken, leading down into a valley where had been much bloody fighting a few months earlier. The small parties united and entered the communicating trenches which led to the front line on another ridge beyond Ribecourt. This ridge overlooked the approach valley to Cambrai which lay on the horizon like the shadow of a cloud.

It was quite dark by the time the relief troops were in the front line taking over from the Hood battalion; luckily the night was calm and the men were able to settle into small dugouts and shelters with a fair measure of comfort. The rum issue was lost, and the soup cold that night, but these matters are of little importance when men are dog-tired. I found two friendly north country chaps to share a small dugout and they fitted in fairly well after careful arrangement of equipment and, apart from occasional disturbances when one or another had to take up sentry duties, we slept soundly until "stand to" in the early morning.

The first streaks of light showed up in the long valley leading towards Cambrai and although it looked very peaceful, almost inviting a walk, it contained hundreds of pairs of eyes looking for a hidden enemy and shooting him immediately he showed a head. Sniping was very fierce in this sector and a large empty biscuit tin placed on the parapet was soon riddled with bullets from unseen rifles.

Charles Straker and Will Harrow, my new pals, were keen to find out where Jerry was as the nearest trenches appeared to be some half mile away down the valley and yet the snipers' rifle shots sounded quite close, so they volunteered to go on a scouting party that night and this is their report as given to me the following night when seated in their dugout over a supper of bully beef, bread and coffee.

"Well Charlie what did you find?" I asked.

"Nothing much for the first ten yards" answered Charlie with deliberation "but Bill nearly fell into a machine gun nest fifty yards away, yelled in surprise and Jerry tried to murder us with a rifle grenade and machine gun fire. We lay doggo for a bit and our officer went on alone for some thirty yards and finding nothing interesting came back for us".

"We had a whispered consultation, lying on our bellies in a dip in the ground, and then some fool of a lance jack suggested exploring the ridge on the left of the valley. Will didn't like the idea and reckoned we were looking for trouble as the sniping always comes from that ridge".

"And I were right" chipped in Will.

"Yes he was" agreed Charlie " we sniffed out three more machine gun posts and two strong points, no trenches anywhere about, and just as the officer gave us the signal for return some damn fool coughed. Talk about fun, we had a firework display and two of our party copped it and we had to drag them back".

"Yes" assented Will "and we found out where Jerry was hiding alright, and if any silly fool wants to know where to find him, just let them walk a hundred yards out to the ridge and cough. He won't need to cough twice".

"Wish I knew who coughed. I'd throttle him".

"Well you wanted some excitement" I suggested "and you found it. Glad you got through alright".

"We got through alright" commented Charlie "but I'm hanged if I hunt for old Jerry any more. That valley and the ridges either side are thick with machine guns, yet there isn't a blinkin' trench in sight".

"The Huns ain't mugs at this game Lofty, and if we had to advance down that peaceful looking valley not one of us would get through".

"Have a smoke you two?" asked Will producing cigarettes. Soon three red ends were glowing and after a short silence a step was heard on the duckboards and a Petty Officer stuck his head in the dugout and asked "Who's in here?".

"Three twots" came the answer.

"Well come out you three twots and join a ration party" sang out the PO with a chuckle and passed swiftly along to the next dugout.

"Well I'm blowed".

"The dirty cow".

"The hound".

Each inhabitant of dugout 43 snapped out these epithets but we obeyed the PO.

"Always bringing up rations" I complained "and seldom getting any".

"Well you see it's all like this" said Charles' sarcastic voice "when they receive our grub at Headquarters its a loaf a man; when it comes up the line, it's half a loaf a man; and by the time it reaches us it's only a fifth each, and if they had many more Quartermasters about we'd not need any ration parties at all!"

"Same with the rum" chipped in Will "I've never seen a chap in the front line drunk yet. In the rear they take it as a drink; in the reserves it's a dose of medicine; but when we get it, why it's only a tooth wash and we still have dirty teeth!"

"Come on, let's go".

It was night, stars were showing faintly through a ground haze, and the Drake battalion was stumbling its weary way back to the old Hindenburg lines behind Ribecourt whose dark forbidding shell-damaged houses gave it an appearance, by night, of a long deserted town whose one time prosperity in life had ebbed away, leaving only its memories to haunt its broken homes.

The Hindenburg Line was a succession of partly smashed trenches running throughout practically the entire battlefront from the English Channel to the Argonne. It marked the long stay in one place that the Germans had made, after the first efforts for Paris in 1914, and subsequent retirement to the Marne strongholds. Its dugouts were deep and well made and only the fact that they faced the enemy lines, when occupied by the British, prevented them from becoming a home of refuge. However, very few direct hits ever occurred and to all purposes they were still very useful for protection and shelter. Some of them could accommodate thirty to forty men with comfort.

To Bill, Charlie and myself the entrance to these trenches spelt duty for, although now in reserve, sentries were posted as in support lines and we three friends were first for duty in our platoon.

The pungent smell of wet earth, cool night air and low diapason notes of distant artillery, combined with a quiet period in gunfire in our sector, made it very difficult to keep awake, so patrolling a portion of the trench, we shared one cigarette between us and kept a sharp lookout for any approaching officer or non-commissioned officer who might object to this breaking of rules.

We were taking the watch of 4am to 6am and, although there was an air of mystery and foreboding about, we little dreamed that the first gas shell which came over at 4.50am and fell with a soft plop behind our trenches was the harbinger of a hail of shells, which drenched our lines with thick fumes, followed by high explosives which smashed our defences to atoms and, as daylight broke, by a low destructive shrapnel barrage. Yet so it happened, and after making sure the first two or three shells were gassy ones and, hearing also a distant alarm, we rang our gas alarms (which were cartridge cases of 6 inch shells) and dived down dugouts at express speed to wake the occupants and see that every man put on his gas helmet.

As the enemy fire grew more intense a general "stand to" was ordered and everyone, looking like denizens of another world, emerged from dugouts like so many ants from a hill, and stood on the firestep straining sleepy eyes to try to peer into the darkness ahead, wondering what was happening to the lads in the front line on the crest of the ridge beyond Ribecourt.

Fury answered fury as our guns answered the enemy, and the indescribable din was making the nerves of the strongest weak almost to breaking point. The enemy were finding our positions with deadly accuracy and the air rang with shouts for stretcher bearers and stretchers.

"This is 'der tag'" shouted Bill to me as we crouched against the parapet.

"What we've been expecting for a long time" I shouted in return.

"Hey Charlie, what's up with Jerry? He's in a nasty temper".

"Must have indigestion Bill" came the cheerful reply.

"Your turn Lofty to take a peep over the top".

I raised my head and peered into the darkness now rent at every second by shell burst or gun flash.

"Can't see a thing" I yelled through my gas helmet.

"This hellish noise is getting on my nerves" growled Bill "shouldn't mind after breakfast, but its damned awful on an empty belly!".

We three relapsed into silence, for it is a rather breathless business talking through a gas helmet.

The dawn came and with it a view of Ribecourt whose freshly heaped ruins told of the intense gunfire of the enemy.

A shouted order was passed along the trench to "put rifle sights at 600 yards and stand by for orders".

"Evidently expecting Jerry to come over the top of that ridge" I thought, examining my rifle at the same time to ascertain that the chamber was fully charged. "I suppose he's captured our front line".

The gunfire quietened down as morning wore on towards midday, gas masks were removed, and famished and thirsty men attacked the rations and tea which had been waiting for some time because one cannot eat with a gas mask covering the head.

"Evidently the Huns, the blighters, are having breakfast on the strength of their attack - they seem quiet enough now" spoke Charlie between mouthfuls of bully beef and bread.

"Wonder how our lads got on in the front line?" queried Bill, producing a few fag ends for his companions' selection.

"Lost 400 yards" chipped in a Petty Officer passing along the trench.

"So that's that" I commented "not such a wonderful start to his boasted big strafe".

"Oh I dunno" replied Bill "can't tell by one day, he's probably advanced five miles elsewhere. I don't think Jerry would waste all those shells for 400 yards of a front line trench".

"Look! look! you chaps" Charlie called excitedly "see that gap in the ridge over there?"

"Good heavens".

"My hat".

"Phew. Millions of them!" "Sure enough Jerry's going to attack again".

An officer came sauntering along the trench and the gap was pointed out to him and also the enemy pouring through the gap and taking up battle positions some 800 yards to the right. Meanwhile the officer's batman was directed post-haste to battalion headquarters to notify the artillery.

"If only our artillery knew".

"Where is their spotter?".

"Asleep I expect".

"Let's have a pot".

"What do you think your rifle is - a howitzer?".

"Bet I could reach them".

"Have a try".

Bill adjusted his sights to full extent and took careful aim. Crack went the rifle and a distant figure stumbled forward.

"Got 'im too".

"Well done Bill".

"More lucky than good" chipped in a near neighbour.

"Don't be damned silly. Bill is a crack shot".

"Let's have a bet on" challenged Bill.

"Done".

Soon many rifles were taking pot shots at the distant enemy and several more men appeared to be hit. The regular pouring of men through the gap ceased for a time but soon began again by rushes of a few at a time.

"Where's the blinkin' artillery?" came an angry remark.

"Gone home".

The sniping went on but still the enemy were coming through the gap.

"That valley in front of us must be lousy with Jerries" said Charlie "and shan't we catch it 'ot to night".

"Tea up" shouted a cook.

For the next fifteen minutes Jerry was left alone and Bill got his teeth into some bread and jam with the remark "Wait 'til I've 'ad my tea you blighters, I'll make you sit up".

132

It was only five minutes later when a few of our guns opened fire on the gap and, after a few good hits, the Germans gave up using that method of dribbling their men through into the valley.

36: Time of reckoning

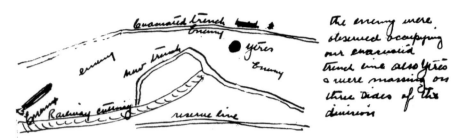

The enemy were observed occupying our evacuated trench line also Ypres & were massing on three sides of the division

Dusk came and stillness reigned over the battlefield, yet thousands of men watched for each other and waited or advanced to kill or be killed.

About 10pm whispered orders were passed along the trenches to move along to the left and form up on the road. In another hour the Drake battalion was preparing to evacuate its position in the Hindenburg line.

An officer came to Bill, Charlie and me, as we were to form part of the rear-guard. "Why are we retiring, sir?" I asked.

"Jerry made five to six miles advance on our right and three miles on our left so our Division must fall back on new positions" answered the officer. "Keep a sharp lookout for Jerry's advance guard and march as quietly as possible, about 300 yards in the battalion rear. Petty Officer Wheatly take charge please".

"Well I'm damned" ejaculated Charles "got to retire have we and not even a smack at Jerry".

The battalion formed up on the road, and like dark shadows moved away into the night; the rear-guard gripped rifles more tightly, with fingers on triggers, and kept watch for some minutes in the eerie darkness until a whispered word from PO Wheatly set the rear-guard on the retreat. The night was very quiet and mysterious save for the soft footfalls of the retreating men bound for an unknown destination. Further along the front guns were beginning to get active but, being some miles away, only dull thuds were heard. Through Metz the troops marched and came to Ruyaulcourt.

Men complained of fatigue. On a retirement there is no thrill of victory to give the men courage, so tired muscles are noticed, and also the unexplained reason for retirement when they had not been beaten. Give the average Englishman a chance for a fight and, if his enemy prove best man, he does not complain but is willing to own defeat for the time until he gets a chance later; but to have to retire without proving who was the better man was bad for his pride.

"Running away from the blighter who ain't beat us" muttered one of my near neighbours.

"Never mind matey, we'll get our chance yet" I answered soothingly.

Suddenly, a whispered "halt" and the column stopped. Officers gave the command to billet and soon our company was billeted in a large YMCA hut. A Sergeant Major appeared and gave the command to sleep fully equipped.

"What's up sir?" asked a voice in the darkness and received the reply "Jerry just down the road and our outposts may be on the move any moment. Don't forget to get a move on if a whistle blows".

"Righto sir", and men, war weary, dirty and thirsty laid down on the hut floor, too tired for conversation or even washing. One lively spirit lit a candle to play cards but finding no companions soon blew out the candle and dropped to sleep.

For four short hours men slept dead and then a sudden entry of the guard shouting "Rouse up here, everybody on the road at once" led to much abuse and swearing as men endeavoured to make a speedy exit yet found helmets missing and accoutrement twisting around their necks at wrong angles. Anyway, the hut cleared itself of its contents in record time. Lining up on the road, cold, shivery and hungry at 5am on a March morning is not conducive to bravery or enthusiasm and when the battalion Commander exhorted them to "Fight to the bitter end at the next defence line" it met with no heroic response, only a stony silence.

Getting on a doorstep he spoke quietly, almost casually "Now men we're up against it and we're falling back to the last defence line this side of the Bapaume-Peronne road. Fight to the bitter end at the next defence line. If we don't stop the Germans now it means defeat for the whole British army. No retiring beyond the next trench line. Fight like Englishmen!"

It was a short march in silence to the position just outside Ytres and no man spoke, except in whispers, until they were in the trenches. A rum issue came along almost immediately, together with the all-important "iron rations", bully beef and biscuits, which served to put new life in the troops.

"Funny thing Charlie, us coming to these trenches, and only a few weeks ago we laughed at the idea of digging so far back" mused Bill.

"Yes, and you said we were digging them for the tourist to see after the war" laughed Charlie. "Can't understand this retirement" I chipped in "it's so quiet and unnatural at times, it doesn't fulfil our idea of war. And who has blundered?"

"Wotcher mean?" asked Bill.

"Why surely some general staff officers must have foreseen this attack and made adequate measures for combating it beforehand?".

"No men, you are wrong" chipped in a quiet voice and turning we saw an officer behind us. "Sorry sir" I apologised.

"Alright old chap, only, you see, the men on our front are only one eighth the number the enemy has in the field and, if we didn't evade him at times and fall back to keep our line, it would mean annihilation of the BEF entirely".

"I see sir" broke in Bill "so we're playing hide and seek?".

"Just for a few hours" answered the officer "and by tomorrow night you'll get all the fighting you want, and perhaps more than you want".

A breathless runner arrived, "Please report headquarters sir" and the officer left immediately.

"Blinkin' good sport that chap" broke in Bill "and he promised us a fight and that sounds good to me".

"You always were a bloodthirsty chap Bill" laughed Charlie.

The morning broke at last, and all throughout the day men stood and waited for the enemy; alarms were frequent, and only the arrival of some ammunition and food broke the strain of waiting.

Some larks rose carolling above the trenches, and the fields were unmarked by shell holes, and the sunshine had quite a mellow warmth in it, added to which was the intense quiet of the whole battle line.

A brooding silence while men marched to Armageddon and eternity, and other men waited to receive them. Hidden hosts nearly at death grips, yet men dozed peacefully on the firestep.

Dusk came on and still no news of the enemy, only ominous gunfire in far south and north. Some figures appeared in the distance and men suddenly became alert and got rifles ready for action, but it was only the outpost screen retiring to the trenches under orders. As the newcomers jumped into the trenches, a sharp exchange of question and answer took place, but all the outposts could report was that a very large body of enemy were advancing from Havringcourt Wood and taking up positions in the valleys near Ruyaulcourt. A solitary airplane flew over our lines towards the east, and later a short burst of shrapnel over the fields 400 yards in front were the only excitements before darkness fell.

Several men came back to the trenches and reported that there were hundreds of cigarettes, much chocolate and biscuits in the church army hut at Ytres, now deserted by the usual salesmen, and then onwards for the next half an hour men in twos and threes paid visits to bring away in sandbags all they could before the enemy should arrive.

At 9pm two men tore back to the trenches and reported they had seen Jerry in Ytres, which lay behind our trenches and, before verification or otherwise could be obtained, the tornado burst in sudden fury. Every enemy gun seemed to play upon the country immediately around Ytres and men clung to the sides of trenches in sudden fear and shock.

This terrific demoralising bombardment lasted half an hour, but seemed like eternity, then the night attack and we survivors of the strafe set to firing in rapid time, and as the enemy masses came on, to using hand grenades, Mills bombs and trench mortars. This fighting for existence lasted only about fifteen minutes, but it was "every man for himself" while it lasted, and Jerry was beaten back for the time being. The trenches were battered to pieces and afforded small shelter for the daybreak attack, which was sure to develop so the command came to retire, and the silence, which had now fallen on the night, was broken only by the groans of dying men, and the quietly whispered orders to evacuate.

To add to the difficulty of retiring the Ytres shell dump blew up[1] and then flared brightly for more than an hour, adding its ghastly light to the scene of carnage, and reflecting in men's faces and showed on them the dazed look of men just emerged from a terrible experience. Luckily for all concerned the enemy did not attack again otherwise the likelihood of any RND men being alive by morning would have been remote.

With worn and weary men set to dig by entrenching tools only, a new defence line was prepared. The chances were greatly in favour of the enemy being able to annihilate us in the early morning, but so well did everyone dig, some even using their hands on the soft mould, that as dawn came most men were in a narrow trench four feet deep and two feet wide with earthworks thrown up to rear and front. Truly a weak position but better than could have been hoped for, in taking together all the circumstances.

1. General Sir H E Blumberg records that is was demolished by Lieutenant T Buckley, 2nd RMLI, under fire; he was awarded the Military Cross

Bill and Charlie lay dead in the old trenches and I, feeling the strain and great loneliness, almost became unmanned, and it was only the thought of all the dear ones depending on me for protection that kept me steady. At 7am,[1] a rum ration came along and a few dry biscuits, after which rifles were cleaned and bayonets fixed for the stern work ahead. The position was as shown in the diagram[2]. The enemy was observed occupying our evacuated trench line, and also Ytres, and were massing on three sides of the Division.

The position seemed untenable, for with no artillery in support and the enemy on three sides, only a miracle could prevent disaster to the Division.

As dawn came and the red sun rose the enemy started sniping, his machine guns fired and he later opened out with his artillery.

The net was closing.

Our officers, the few who were left, encouraged the men by walking along the top, heedless of enemy bullets. A foolhardy thing to do, but it gave confidence to everyone especially as they were unhit by the enemy. Every man now had three days' growth of beard, were worn with fatigue and faces streaked with sweat, but all the same most were hardened warriors and grim of countenance. These officers and men had been victorious in many a fight and had also taken a licking at times, but with their backs to the wall they were prepared to give Jerry a good fight. Pride of race, blood and tradition came uppermost, and where one or two showed signs of nerves the officers bucked them up.

'B' Company officer stopped his prowling opposite one such man and said in a firm tone "I want a good man to volunteer for a risky job. What about you?"

It mastered the man's nerves immediately and he volunteered and with several others, me among them, we went across 'no man's land' to take up defensive positions in the railway cutting. Action pulled the weak ones together, it being the terrible strain of waiting that wears the nerves.

The firing gradually grew more intense, and nerves almost reached breaking point, when the enemy came out of their trenches and our men opened fire taking careful aim, machine guns kept up their regular fire, Lewis guns spat, and the enemy lines dissolved. Thus ended the first attack.

1. On 24 March 1918
2. At this chapter head

138

The second soon started and was even more determined in character; the enemy reserves were fast coming up in support and even his light artillery was firing direct into our trenches on open sights. What made the position worse was the need to economise in ammunition, as the supply parties had ceased to operate and only the bullets contained in each man's pouches were to be relied upon. Also all our artillery had withdrawn owing to enemy outposts threatening to cut our communications in the rear.

The second attack developed and feverishly our boys sent up SOS signals for artillery assistance but none came, and only when the Germans were 150 yards away was the order to fire given to the infantry. The next five minutes was furious work and grim, but the defence held and, despite the absence of barbed wire in front of our trenches, no enemy ever reached our lines. The attack melted away and our boys were able to rest a bit.

"Phew, what a scrap" muttered one man wiping his forehead with a dirty bit of rag which served as handkerchief and rifle cleaner.

"How many more rounds you got left?" asked his neighbour.

"Fifteen only mate, and then it's all up."

"I've only twelve, so if Jerry attacks again it finishes my supply."

"Where's the bloody artillery?"

"Gone shopping" chipped in another.

"How many blokes we lost?"

"Nigh on thirty I reckon, and can't bury one of 'em yet."

"Hello! What's the row in the cutting?"

An officer yelled out "Twenty men in the cutting quick. Jerry's coming down it."

A score ran and ducked to the cutting to support me and my party and for ten short, sharp minutes a splendid scrap took place, but again the enemy made no headway, only gained a hold of about forty yards at the extreme end of the cutting and at a cost of some sixty to seventy men. Eleven of our boys lay dead and the Lewis gun out of ammunition.

I sent two men to report to the officer of the Company, if he was still alive, and meanwhile the survivors loaded rifles and lay in wait.

The third attack developed on our trenches and this time the enemy attacked from two sides and came shouting and waving out of his trenches. Our boys yelled back and then again the firing for dear life, and with bullets running short our men had only about half the volume of fire. The Germans, by short rushes, got to within striking distance when an officer suddenly jumped on the parapet and shouted "Let them have your bombs men and charge the blighters".

Our thin line came out on top and cursing and shouting at the Germans we flung our bombs and started in to attack with bayonet, but the enemy had lost their nerve after the rain of bombs and they broke before the sudden onslaught and fled to their trenches; it was only the strong command of our few surviving officers which restrained our men and sent them back to the shelter of the trenches.

"We give them Huns hell 'eh mate?"

"Yes we did, but no good giving chase with no ammo left, we should have been wiped out".

"Never mind we made the bleeders run, and they won't forget it for a bit!".

Hardly had our men resumed their trenches to await the inevitable massacre, for the Germans were sending fresh masses across the fields to attack and were also developing the attack north and south of Ytres, when a sudden order came to retire.

"The enemy has broken through our flanks men so get out quick" roared an officer's voice above the din of the enemy artillery "Every man for himself". The confusion that followed beggars description. The enemy brought every machine gun into the open fields around and our boys had to run the gauntlet. It was hell with the lid off, and after running and walking some three thousand yards most of the men dumped themselves into shell holes too exhausted for further movement. Three days and nights of strenuous retirement with only seven good hours of sleep and very little food, with a gallant fight all the morning of the 24 March against odds of 6 to 1, plus the fact of only a few rounds of ammunition left in their pouches rendered our division practically at the mercy of the enemy; and then the call for a strong run and a long run leaves little cause for wonder that a number should turn and dump themselves into shell holes to await a suitable time to surrender. Many still went on firing the few remaining cartridges left but all to no avail with the enemy completely encircling them.

I and my small party in the railway cutting did not receive the order to retire and it was only when one of us saw some of our men retiring across the fields in the distance that we realised our plight. After a run through a hail of bullets from both enemy and friends, we took refuge in a small newly dug trench and continued to snipe at the approaching enemy advance parties until our ammunition had gone.

Our division left hundreds of dead[1] lying about in grotesque shapes and attitudes upon the fields of Ytres, and only a small remnant of the reserves made good their escape from the German pincer movement. A tragic retirement, but gallant and of inestimable value to our army in the delay that it caused to the German advance.

And yet some cads at home, secure in club armchairs, had the impudence to criticise the Fifth Army Corps.

Ye Gods!!

Their fat stomachs would have shaken with fear at the sound of the first bullet whining through the air.

The German advance parties rounded up the few prisoners remaining alive and on stepping out of my trench I observed in the far distance the still retiring figures of the khaki-clad army of Britain in full retreat before the German hordes, and the sight sickened me.

During the afternoon Barastre, Rocquigny, LeTransloy, Beaulencourt, Gueudecourt, Flers and even Bapaume fell to the enemy and only nightfall enabled the shattered 5th Army Corps to reform.

The Germans had suffered heavily in the advance and the few hours of quiet enabled them to reform and bring up further fresh reserves in guns and men. One of the wonderful sights was to see their transport and guns following upon the heels of the infantry, and keeping up the formation and lines of communication so vital to an advancing army.

---

1. In the month following 21 March 1918, the start of the German Offensive, 'Operation Michael', the British sustained 250,000 casualties – as many as those at Passchendaele

There ends my father's manuscript of his war experiences.
He was posted "Killed in action, 25th March 1918", during the strong German offensive, Operation Michael, launched on 21 March. His parents (my grandparents) mourned the death of their only offspring for six weeks until the military informed them that a postcard had been received from Frederick Cornelius, stating that he was a prisoner-of-war at Limburg an der Lahn (a small medieval town some 25 miles east of Koblenz). The amazement and joy of his parents can scarcely be imagined.
My father recorded nothing of his eight months as a prisoner-of-war in the prison camps at Limburg an der Lahn and then Gustrow, Mecklenburg to which he had been transferred. Perhaps it was a time of shame, trauma and deprivation too difficult for him to deal with.
He was repatriated weighing only seven stone and attributed his survival to the ministrations of, and food from, local Nuns and the availability of little green apples in spring and early summer from the orchards near the camp.
DFC

Site of prisoner of war camp, Limburg an der Lahn

REMEMBRANCE

Fourteen Years Later. Empire Day, 1932

The lonely figure of a man stands on the cliff top at Folkestone looking out over the sea to where the coast of France shows dimly in the distance. He can hear again the voices of men, now lying dead over there, he communes with them in spirit. A shaft of sunshine like a gigantic searchlight lights up the white cliffs of France for a moment, and he remembers again the landing at Boulogne, the dull booming of the guns in their death grips, and hears the shrieks and groans of torn men in their agony. One million of our dead 'over there' - the sunlight fades.

The lone figure returns to the Road of Remembrance - it leads down to the harbour, a stone altar stands at the top of the road and inscribed thereon:

He stands bareheaded for the road is a Holy Road and our dead lie in line from the sea to Mons.
The road to the harbour, millions of laughing, gay young men departed to and from this harbour, and millions more left in sadness - came back in agony; and one million - never came back.

The note of a bird breaks the reverie, a similar note saved madmen on the other side.

Now it is Peace, thank God, and if the lonely figure knows that the real Peace has not yet dawned on mankind, at least he has his memories of those who did their bit to bring Peace to mankind.

Greater love hath no man than this
that he lay down his life for his friends.
At the going down of the sun,
and in the morning,
We will remember them.

144

FURTHER READING

BARNETT (C) The Great War. Park Lane Press. 1979. 116pp.

BLUMBERG (General Sir H E) Britain's Sea Soldiers. A Record of the Royal Marines during the war. 1914-19. Swiss & Co. Devonport 1927.

BROWN (M) Tommy goes to War. J M Dent & Sons Ltd. London. 1978. ISBN 0 460 02220 2

COOMBS (Rose E B) Before Endeavours Fade. Battle of Britain Prints International Ltd. London. 1990. (6th Ed). ISBN 0 900913 62 2.

EVANS (Martin Marix) The Battles of the Somme. Wiedenfeld and Nicolson. London. 1996. ISBN: 0 297 83587 4.

GILES (John) Flanders - Then and Now. (3rd Ed). After the Battle. 1986. 208pp. ISBN: 0 900913 48 7.

GILES (John) The Somme - Then and Now . (2nd Ed) After the Battle. 1986. 176pp. ISBN: 0 900913 41 X.

HARRIS (J) The Somme: Death of a generation. Hodder & Stoughton Ltd. 1966. 128pp.

JERROLD (D) The Royal Naval Division. Hutchinson & Co. London. 1923.

JERROLD (D) The Hawke Battalion 1914-18. Benn. London. 1925.

KINGSMILL (H) Behind Both Lines. Morley & Mitchell. London. 1930.

MACDONALD (Lyn) Somme. Book Club Associates and Michael Joseph Ltd. 1983.

MAIR (C) Britain at war 1914-19. John Murray (Publisher) Ltd. 1982. 122pp. ISBN 0 7195 3877 7.

MURRAY (Joseph) Call to Arms – From Gallipoli to The Western Front. William Kimber and Company Limited. London 1980. 191pp ISBN 0 7183 0097 4.

NETTLETON (J) The Anger of the Guns. William Kimber & Co Ltd. London. 1979. ISBN 0 7183 0316 4.

SPARROW (G) AND ROSS (J N M) On Four Fronts with the Royal Naval Division Hodder & Stoughton. London. 1918.

SHERMER (David) World War 1. Octopus Books Ltd. London. 1973. ISBN: 0 7064 0245 6.

TERRAIME (J) The First World War 1914-18. Hutchinson & Co (Publisher) Ltd. 1965. 195pp. ISBN 0 436 51730 2.

WINTER (J M) The Experience of World War I. Macmillan London Ltd, 1988. 256pp. ISBN 0 333 4461 3.

VAN EMDEN (Richard) Prisoners of the Kaiser. Pen and Sword Military 2000. ISBD 978 1 848840 78 2

FMN Cornelius' Service Record

MINISTRY OF DEFENCE
Bourne Avenue Hayes Middlesex UB3 1RF

Telephone   081-57-33831 ext **341**

Mr D F Cornelius
White Poplars
Webb Lane
Hayling Island
Hampshire
PO11 9JE

Your reference

Our reference
ROH 3210/91/RC

Date
2 October 1991

Dear Mr Cornelius

Re: F M N CORNELIUS

Thank you for your enquiry requesting details from your father's service record while serving in the Royal Naval Division during the First World War.

We have successfully traced his record but this contains only a brief outline of his service and it would appear that most of these details are already known to you from the manuscript in your possession.

From the documents we hold we have extracted the only details remaining of your father's service.

FULL NAME: Frederick Marcus Nightingale CORNELIUS

DATE OF BIRTH: 8 June 1896

Enlisted at the Royal Naval Division Recruiting Office, 112 The Strand, WC, on 12 November 1915 to serve for the duration of the war in the Royal Naval Volunteer Reserve, London Division and allocated the official service number LZ/4013.

FULL ADDRESS: Lynmouth, 17 Beverley Road, Highams Park, Essex

TRADE OR CALLING
AND IN WHOSE
EMPLOY: Shipping Clerk   Messrs Gerhard & Hey Ltd
                                      1/3 Gt St Thomas Apostle
                                      EC

NEXT OF KIN: (Father) F G CORNELIUS

PERSONAL DESCRIPTION
ON ENTRY: Height: 6ft 0 in, Chest: 35½ in,
                                Hair: Brown, Eyes: Brown

PERSONAL MARKS: Small mole left elbow, chickenpox scars left abdomen

NATURE OF ANY
SEA EXPERIENCE: None (cannot swim)

147

The following entries are as recorded on your father's record card:

20 November 1915	Attached to 4th Battalion
10 January 1916	Returned from Signal School to 4th Battalion
14 April 1916	Drafted from 4th Battalion Depot, to 1st Reserve Battalion, Blandford
May 1916	Attached to 2nd Drake Battalion B Company
10 July 1916	Transferred from 2nd Drake Battalion to Howe Battalion (British Expeditionary Forces) embarked Folkestone disembarked Boulogne
12 July 1916	Joined 63rd (RN) Division Base Depot Etaples
20 August 1916	Joined Howe Battalion in Field
16 September 1916	To Second Field Ambulance (Septic right heel) to hospital
18 September 1916	To 6th Casualty Clearing Station
26 September 1916	To No 31 Ambulance Train
27 September 1916	Admitted to 20 General Hospital, Dannes Camiers
11 October 1916	To 6th Convalescence Depot Etaples
31 October 1916	Admitted to 24th General Hospital Etaples (Influenza)
31 October 1916	To 6th Convalescence Depot Etaples
13 November 1916	To Base Depot Calais
19 November 1916	Rejoined Unit (Howe Battalion)
20 October 1917 to	30 October 1917 Leave to UK
1 November 1917	Rejoined Unit
28 February 1918	Joined 7th Entrenching Battalion
14 March 1918	Posted to Drake Battalion
25 March 1918	Report received from Base "Killed in action 25 March 1918" Next-of-kin informed
7 May 1918	PC received from rating stating prisoner of war at Kriegsgefangenen - Kommandantur Wahn, Limburg A/Lahn N-o-K informed
3 June 1918	Previously reported killed in action now posted as missing and prisoner of war in German hands
13 August 1918	PM List 481. GEFLG Gustrow from Western Front
25 November 1918	Admitted 2 Canadian Casualty Clearing Station
26 November 1918	Admitted 51 Casualty Clearing Station
29 November 1918	Admitted 3 Canadian General Hospital Boulogne
30 November 1918	Repatriated prisoner of war arrived at Dover
27 January 1919	Reported to 2nd Reserve Battalion
6 February 1919	Demobilised (Purfleet)

RATINGS HELD: Ordinary Seaman to Able Bodied Seaman

Your father's medal entitlement was, the Victory Medal and the British War Medal. It is recorded that these were presented to him.

The Royal Naval Division were men belonging to the Reserves of the Royal Navy who were surplus to requirements on board ships, but held on land bases for any special purpose for which they might be needed by the Admiralty. They were used throughout the First World War and were included among the most famous divisions of the British Army although still keeping their naval origins and practices.

The author's home at Beverley Road, Highams Park, Essex from
which he went to war

Marine Crescent, Folkestone. The billet from which the author and
thousands of others embarked for France

150

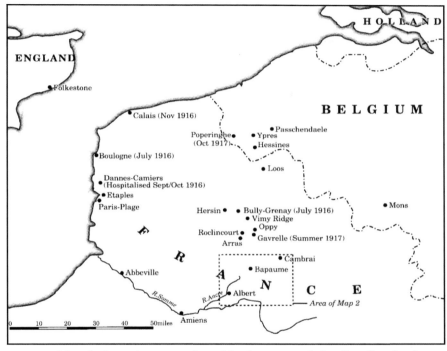

Map 1: Locations mentioned in the text and details of author's posngs

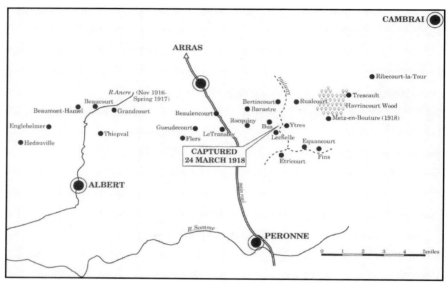

Map 2: Somme-Ancre-Cambrai sector where the author served
during November 1916 to Spring 1917 and Spring 1918

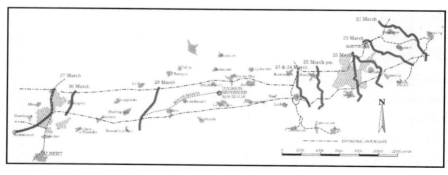

Map 3: Royal Naval Division Sector during German Offensive,
March 1918 A simplified map. Original: Douglas Jerrold. The Royal
Naval Division. Hutchinson & Co. London 1923

German front line Beaumont Hamel (photographed 1991)

Allied trenches, Beaumont Hamel (photographed 1991)

Memorial crosses at the prisoner of war camp, Limburg an der Lahn

Prisoner of war camp, Gustrow - Photographs courtesy of Norbert Haertle

Frederick Marcus Nightingale Cornelius & Florence Kate Allen

Fourteen years later the author with his children - August, 1932

Post Script

In 2009 the last three British warriors of World War 1 passed away, thereby severing totally our direct human links to that cataclysmic event. Despite the thread of person-to-person continuity being broken, we still have film, photographs and written accounts of WW1. This book, "Path of Duty", is one such.

My father recorded his experiences whilst serving with the Royal Naval Division (RND) on the Western Front, but he was totally unforthcoming about his eight months as a Prisoner-of-War (PoW). So it was with a great deal of curiosity and the help of an archivist at the local Rathaus (Town Hall) that my wife and I visited in 1993 the site of the PoW camp at Limburg an der Lahn, (a delightful medieval town some 25 miles east of Koblenz) where my father is first recorded as being held; the camp is about 250 miles east of where he was captured near Ytres.

But it was not until 2005, five years after the publication of "Path of Duty" that we visited Gustrow (some 30 miles south of the port and seaside town of Warnemunde) in Mecklenburg where he was held for at least three months as a PoW and maybe rather more. Here again, we visited the Rathaus and studied its limited archived information on the PoW camp. This information referred to Herr Norbert Haertle of Gustrow who owned documents, an album of photographs of the PoW camp and artefacts made by the prisoners of war. We made contact with him at his home.

The album of photographs of the 1914/15 period show the PoW camp to be large, substantial and international in character, there being photos of British, French, Australian, Russian, Italian, Indian and African soldiers. The various camp facilities included a laundry, bakery, disinfection equipment, washrooms, Catholic church, Russian church, hospital, carpentry workshops and so on. The overall impression is of well-fed prisoners, relaxing, smoking, socializing, with music and hobby activities and generally living well-organized lives as prisoners of war. In fact they were prisoners with no prospect of release in the foreseeable future; they were subject to random discipline from the guards; they were little more than slave labour in the working parties, and they lived on the minimum of food which would get less in the years to come – approaching starvation level as the Allied food blockade took effect later in the war. The memorials and very many individual graves are a measure of a high death rate for the PoWs. The site of this camp is now a civil/leisure airport and this fact gives some idea of its size.

I was 25 years old when my father died aged 61. Like most young men in their twenties, I was pre-occupied with carving a career, with a young wife and a marriage of little more than one year at the time of my father's death. The traumatic and horrifying things that happened to my father between his ages of 19 and 22, was not something we had ever discussed. It was some 30 years later when I first read and transcribed his writings into "Path of Duty" that I regretted bitterly, and still do to this day, not having asked him about his writings and the wartime experiences that they represented. He would have been able to answer all the questions that crowded into my mind about his service life and his written account of it. For example, why did he write it in the third person, giving himself a pseudonym? Was it too painful to write of the three years of war and captivity in the first person? What were the real names of his fellow warriors? – research into the names by which he referred to them - Jack Ferris, Bob Martyn and so on – fail to show up in the MoD records and the internet. When did he write the book? His wife, Florence, was unaware of his writing it. They were married in 1927 so there is an eight year period between his eventual discharge from the RND and his marriage to Florence Allen when he could have penned his wartime experiences.

The emotional distance between those fighting on the Western Front and those at home is well documented. This separation arises from the fighting man's reluctance to talk about conditions in the front line, maybe to shield those he loved from the brutalities and horror of trench warfare, or from an inability to convey a realistic picture of the sub-human conditions under which the sweethearts, husbands, fathers and sons of those at home lived and fought. The civilian population received, in the main, anodyne or gung-ho reports of the fighting through the press; there was nothing like the news coverage that today's conflicts attract. And censorship of letters to home sealed another potential source of information.

Those at home, therefore, generally had a rosy view of the war, fed by limited or mis-information from journalists who relied on news about campaigns fed to them by those in command relatively remote from the front line, a location to which it appears journalists were not permitted access initially. One has only to read the triumphant account of temporary territorial gains of a few hundred yards at a cost of thousands of casualties, before it was lost again to enemy counter attacks, to realize how impoverished was the quality of the reporting.

My father's account well describes the trench and battle conditions that he encountered as he took supplies (food, munitions, materiel) by horse transport to the front line by day and night. But what he does not describe after his capture was how the prisoners were treated. Remember, this was March 1918 when the German civil population was suffering starvation following effective blockades by the Allies; a situation likely to create hostility by guards towards prisoners.

There are so many unanswered questions, beginning with how he and other prisoners were taken the 250 miles from Ytres to Limburg an der Lahn; marched? by road or rail transport? The site of the Limburg PoW camp is some 5 miles outside the town. It is still in a walled location in the open countryside, and within the walls are memorials to the Ulster Regiment, to the Russian dead, and individual graves to those of other nationalities. Were the soldiers required to work? and if so, what type of work and for how long each day?
What proportion of prisoners were fit or wounded?
How many of the RND died in captivity at this camp through wounds or other causes?

Similar questions apply to the PoW camp at Gustrow, some 320 miles to the north-east of Limburg an der Lahn. Were the prisoners marched or transported by road or rail? Did they have to work? How many died due to wounds, illness or other causes?
What news, if any, did they receive on the progress of the war? How often could my father receive and send letters? And what news could they contain? Were their letters censored by the British or German authorities?

In World War I over 170,000 British soldiers were taken prisoner, some 72,000 during the German offensive "Operation Michael" in March 1918 when my father was captured.

In his book "Prisoners of the Kaiser" Richard van Emden answers many of the above questions. He discovered, by interviewing over twenty ex-PoWs, all over 100 years old, the range of their experiences on the shock and terror of capture; their treatment and feelings as they were consolidated as PoWs; the quality and quantity of their rations and the hunger they endured; the ill-treatment suffered; their fears for the future; the work that they were obliged to do; and how they were marched to, for example, railheads where they were transported by cattle trucks on long journeys with little or no food and no facilities. Their replies would no doubt encapsulate some experiences that my father also underwent. These include his rare spoken comments: about the treatment meted out by the guards...." the younger guards were always harsher disciplinarians than the older guards"; about food... "we were always hungry and were kept alive by the kindnesses and food given by local Nuns and the apples we were able to gather from the trees in spring and summer from orchards near the camp", so clearly he was involved in working parties outside the wire. He returned home weighing only seven stone, even though he was over six feet tall.

After the Armistice of 11 November 1918 the handover of prisoners was haphazard, depending on where they were held and the way the handover was organised by the local prison Commandant. In my father's case, it was two weeks *after* the end of the war before he was admitted on 25 November to 2 Canadian Casualty Clearing Station, and the following day to 51 Casualty Clearing Station. Three more days passed before he reached, on 29 November, the 3 Canadian General Hospital, Boulogne. So it was not until 30 November that he eventually arrived at Dover as a repatriated prisoner of war. Humanely, the government granted repatriated prisoners two months home leave to allow them time to re-integrate with their families and, in my father's case, and no doubt many others, to return gradually to wholesome food and normal diets and the chance to build up their abused bodies.

He finally reported to 2nd Reserve Battalion on 27 January 1919 and was demobilized on 6 February, so ending his war, his Path of Duty, some 3 years 2 months 3 weeks and 4 days after the date of his enlistment.

My father had left his tightly knit Victorian-style family at age 19 and returned after three years of service life, having been a part of the violence and slaughter of trench warfare, seeing his friends and fellow soldiers killed, gassed and horrifically wounded, and then spending eight months as a prisoner of war. His experiences as a young man in France during the Great War seared themselves on my father's mind. His reactions to the outbreak of the Second World War were of despair and a sense of betrayal by politicians. He hated war and its glorification and would have nothing to do with 'victory' celebrations thereafter.

One can only guess what a huge effort would have been required by Frederick and his parents to achieve the process of his rehabilitation into family life and society in general. Possibly as a part of this he began to write his story as, consciously or unconsciously, he sought to provide the therapy necessary to purge the images of war and to pave the way for re-entry to a stable civilian lifestyle. Whenever his tale was written, it was undoubtedly successful in this way as evidenced by his return to work, the restoration of normal social activities, marriage eventually and the raising of a family.

DFC – 2014

Frederick Cornelius: Forty years on, 1918 – 1958

After demobilization Frederick returned to his old job as a shipping clerk, firstly with Gerhard and Hey Ltd and then with Lep Transport at Tilbury whilst he lived with his parents in Highams Park.

Nine years later, he married Florence Kate, fourth daughter of David and Fanny Allen, on 23 April 1927 and they spent their honeymoon in Devon. They visited Dawlish where his father was born and previous generations of his family lived and worked as owners and printers of "The Dawlish Gazette".

On return to Essex they rented a semi-detached house in Highams Park, and later a terraced Victorian house in Woodford Green. During these ten years Frederick continued his employment as a shipping clerk, though he cast his eyes around for self-employment opportunities to enhance his income now that he had a family of four to support; but he had little success in finding the right opportunity.

In 1937 the family moved to a small bungalow in Thundersley, Essex from where his daughter and son attended Hadleigh Junior and Infant schools, respectively, and the family worshipped at Hadleigh Methodist Church. Then came WW2 and the "phoney war" which lasted until early

May 1940 when the air raids began. Frederick, in common with many others, erected an Anderson air raid shelter in his garden. Thundersley, on the Thames Estuary, was in the flight path of the German bombers, and therefore received its share of the night-time air raids.

Following his experiences of WW1, and wishing to remove his family as far as possible from any conflict, Frederick self-evacuated his family in May 1940 to Dawlish where he hoped they would be safe. He found office work in Plymouth and travelled daily from Dawlish. But this idyllic life was rudely shattered when Plymouth became the target for German bombs in a series of air raids culminating in the major blitz in March 1941. In the post-blitz chaos it was not possible for Frederick to communicate with his wife, so until he was able to return home the following day, his family feared the worst, but thankfully this was not so.

After the extensive bomb damage in Plymouth changed the working pattern of that city, Frederick was either transferred to, or found work in, Exeter. Although it had suffered the occasional small air raid, Exeter was as safe a place to work as any other city. But it was not to remain so and in May 1942 it suffered a severe blitz on a scale similar to that experienced by Plymouth. The sky over Exeter glowed red with the reflected light of fires in the city as it was extensively bombed and this red glow could be seen from Frederick's home in Dawlish.

Although physically unharmed, Frederick was a casualty in a different way. The cumulative effect of his experiences in WW1, and his involvement in the blitzes in Plymouth and Exeter damaged his nerves and restricted his ability and willingness to undertake work in cities and large towns. He thus turned his hand from the cerebral work in offices to the physical work of the gardener/handyman in rural locations.

His first foray into such work led him to Luppitt, some three miles outside Honiton, where he worked for, and on the large estate of, Major General and Lady Osborne. Frederick was provided with a cottage with an outside toilet, no bathroom (hip baths in front of the living room fire were *de riguer*), no electricity, no gas, but paraffin lamps and a large kitchen range. For many, an idyllic rural set-up, but not for Florence – an ordinary suburban housewife used to cooking by gas, electric light, indoor toilets and a bathroom!

The estate had a pony and trap and Frederick loved caring for, grooming and feeding the pony, whilst no doubt re-living his WW1 experiences with his horses with which he shared mortal danger almost every day of his time in France and Belgium. He even took his family shopping in Honiton in the pony and trap – a round trip of some six miles. Frederick's daughter and son revelled in this rural life with its open-air freedom, involvement with tree felling and the splitting of tree trunks, collecting duck and chicken eggs, the abundance of play space and the pleasurable three mile cycle ride to school along country lanes and a wartime-quiet main road.

However despite these idyllic aspects, the downside of this work was the primitive living conditions. So after three months, with winter approaching, Frederick left; a move probably welcomed by Florence who found it difficult to adapt to the basic rural facilities.

But Frederick still needed the ambience that this type of work offered his troubled nerves, so he found work with the Rector of St. Petrock's Anglican Church in Lydford, a small village between Okehampton and Tavistock in Devon. Lydford boasts a castle and a gorge, visitor attractions nowadays, but not in the wartime 40's. Frederick's work included operating the boiler and heating system to keep the church warm, and all things to do with maintaining the church grounds, grass, trees and hedges in good condition.

Again, Florence had to cook on a kitchen range, but here there were the luxuries of electric light, a bathroom and an inside toilet. Once again, three months was the job duration before Frederick left, though the reason was unknown to his offspring.

He returned to Dawlish where he lived for the rest of his life. During this time he rented a second floor Victorian flat in the centre of the town convenient for beaches, lawns, church, shops, station, cinema and library. This time, Florence had all mod. con! Some two years later Frederick was able to rent a modern two-bedroomed bungalow about one mile out of town towards Exeter. A few years later he was offered the chance to buy the bungalow as a sitting tenant, and this he did; it was his home until he died.

Following his return to Dawlish, Frederick undertook various activities in the community, based almost entirely on the Congregational (now United Reformed) church of which he was a staunch member. Early on he joined the church choir and was subsequently followed by all members of his family. Then as needs arose in the Sunday school he became their Superintendent for a number of years; likewise, when the choirmaster resigned he willingly undertook this role, music being his passion - he always owned and played a harmonium. For many years he was a member of the Diaconate that assisted the Minister in leading the church in matters spiritual and material. Frederick revelled in these activities – they were his life and joy.

His working life encompassed several and various types of work as he slowly recovered from his Blitz experiences. He was an outgoing, affable person, able easily to establish rapport with those whom he met. This defined, not surprisingly, the types of work he felt able to undertake. Early during this period he worked in the office of Miloko of Crediton, manufacturers of milk by-products. But travelling was difficult on a daily basis in wartime so when opportunity presented itself he became a local agent for the Prudential Assurance Company with all that that entailed in person-to-person contact.

Subsequently, Frederick was attracted to commercial travelling as an occupation, working for various employers, mainly on commission, which did not bring in much income during these war years nor for several years afterwards. During these times austerity reigned and manufacturing was concentrated on more important areas of activity to help aid national economic recovery, rather than the luxury goods market that Frederick seemed destined to focus upon. Thus one company whom he represented marketed cameras, compasses, opera glasses and such things optical, but prices were high and demand was low so eventually he moved towards ladies toiletries of various types. These had a high demand factor, but money was in short supply so again it was a struggle to sell.

Transport was difficult for Frederick, as he had no driving licence or car. His solution was to carry his samples, thankfully small, in a suitcase on the pannier of his bicycle, and to take his bike by train to whichever town he wished to visit where he would cycle between the selling places at each destination. This system of travel gave him flexibility and a good range of territory, and he stayed away overnight, when necessary, to maximize his time in town.

As Frederick got older, the nature of the work he was doing became more difficult to hold down so that he was deemed "too old at 55". Money became short and life became hard, but his wife took in summer visitors and did other temporary work to help with the family budget, whilst he found whatever work he could, menial or otherwise, to keep them barely afloat financially; they struggled on, helped when possible by their offspring.

Then at age 59 Frederick received the cruel diagnosis of lung cancer. He declined treatment and fought this disease with fortitude, nursed entirely by Florence. He lost weight steadily, until he passed away peacefully and without pain in his own bed on 6 March 1958, aged 61 years. He is interred in Dawlish Cemetery with Florence who died in 1982.

In his Last Will and Testament Frederick wrote;

"Unto my wife, my very great love for all she has been to me and her selfless work and companionship and to my son and daughter my deep appreciation of their love and loyalty. God bless all richly and keep you safe until we meet again".